A Divine Mercy Resource

How to Understand the Devotion to Divine Mercy

Richard "Rick" Torretto

iUniverse, Inc.
New York Bloomington

A Divine Mercy Resource
How to Understand the Devotion to Divine Mercy

iUniverse books may be ordered through booksellers or by contacting:

iUniverse
1663 Liberty Drive
Bloomington, IN 47403
www.iuniverse.com
1-800-Authors (1-800-288-4677)

ISBN: 978-1-4502-3236-4 (pbk)
ISBN: 978-1-4502-3237-1 (cloth)
ISBN: 978-1-4502-3238-8 (ebk)

Printed in the United States of America

Library of Congress Control Number: 2010929444

iUniverse rev. date: 6/7/2010

www.SolomonsCourt.com
solomonscourt@aol.com

Front Cover: The Original Vilnius Image of Divine Mercy painted by Eugene Kazimierowski under the direction of Saint Faustina. Courtesy Life Foundation Ministries, Bernalillo, NM.

Contents

Dedication

This book is dedicated to my loving bride of 47 years, Penny. In March 1963, she was introduced to a young Catholic Army Captain who fell madly in love with her. She trusted and agreed to marry him and did so on May 25, 1963.

She is not only my bride, the mother of our children (four beautiful daughters), but also my prayer partner, soul mate, confidant, and lightening rod (intercessor).

When I was retiring from the United States Army and announced I was getting a Masters in Theology, although she knew it wasn't going to put food on the table or money in the bank account, she trusted and supported me.

Now many years later, able to speak intimately on *"for better or worse, for richer or poorer, in sickness and health,"* having experienced them all, she still trusts in her bridegroom (who is much older and wiser now), and awaits with excitement what new adventure God holds in store for us.

Thank you Penny for helping me to truly understand and experience the grace of the Sacrament of Marriage, and what "Jesus, I trust in you," entails.

Acknowledgements

The publication of a book involves many people besides the author. Such is the case with A *Divine Mercy Resource (How to Understand the Devotion to Divine Mercy)*.

Therefore, I begin by acknowledging Fr. Leo Phillips, C.S.V., at whose feet (literally) I studied Greek for two years as his only student; and Fr. Charles Miller, S.M., my advisor and professor of theology at St. Mary's University, San Antonio, Texas, who relentlessly insisted I study Hebrew. These two professors gave me a love of these languages that continues to grow each day.

Sister Josephine Boyles, O.S.F., who, when she first heard me speak at a local seminar, took me under her broad shoulders, guided, pushed and focused me into a teaching and apologetics ministry, and continues to be my mentor, personal friend, and greatest loving critic. Many thanks to the *Sisters of St. Francis of the Holy Eucharist* in Independence, Missouri, who always generously and graciously provided a forum for talks, conferences, retreats, and seminars.

I thank Kathleen Keefe, founder of *"Peace Through Divine Mercy,"* who heard me as the emcee and speaker at a Kansas conference and recommended me as emcee and speaker for the first Divine Mercy Conference in San Francisco in 1993. The organizer, Thelma Orias, accepted me, and trusted. These two evangelists of Divine Mercy continue to be great friends and supporters.

Thelma Orias took a chance on me and California became my speaking forum for eight conferences in six years causing me to study and understand Divine Mercy in new ways. It was at the Los Angles Divine Mercy Conference in 1996 that Robert Stackpole, Research Director of the John Paul II Institute of Divine Mercy, Stockbridge, MA, heard me and recommended that Fr. Seraphim Michalenko, M.I.C., the director, invite me as a speaker for their seminars and conferences. In January 1999, I presented a theological essay at the first North American Symposium of the John Paul II Institute of Divine Mercy, in Washington, D.C. That essay is Chapter 8 of this book.

No one can succeed in any ministry without outstanding prayer warriors who stand in the gap and intercede. With the possibility of forgetting someone I would nevertheless like to publicly acknowledge, Gregoria Gamon, Virginia Irvine, Trudy Compton, Sue Lee, Charlotte Lesslie, Mother Charlotte Mary of Agape House, Sam and Nancy Jones, and Kathleen Sheehan.

I cannot forget Deacon Kenneth Hill, from my home parish. He has always tried to advance my teaching ministry and continues to be a great friend and supporter.

And a special thanks to Christian and Marya Reedy, also from my home parish. They joined us on our 2006 Holy Land Pilgrimage and became close personal and spiritual friends. I am indebted that they have financially assisted in publishing this book.

Special thanks to Monsignor Douglas A. Raun, St. Thomas Aquinas Parish, Rio Rancho, NM, my pastor, for his personal friendship, advice, and dauntless support of my ministry. He has given me an open forum through the parish's Adult Catholic Theology Series (ACTS).

Special thanks to Elizabeth Hackett, *Life Foundation Ministries*, who gave me my full size Original Vilnius Image of Divine Mercy. She has become a personal friend, advisor and co-worker. Also, Tim McAndrews, *Laity for Mercy*, a co-worker, prayer warrior and supporter of my ministry.

I owe a personal debt to Jim Cope, a true friend, who when no one else believed in my mission, continued to encourage, cajole and push me to persevere.

Most importantly, to Mary, Queen, Mother of Mercy, and my mother, who has kept me safe and secure under her Blue Mantle and whispers in my soul constantly, "Do whatever He tells you."

Introduction

Why another book on Divine Mercy and a resource at that?

When I first began to speak and teach on the Mercy of God I said I felt fulfilled because it brought together all the studies and events in my life through which God directed me into this meaningful mission: Proclaiming and publishing the Good News of His Divine Mercy.

For over 20 years I have been privileged to tour the country giving talks, retreats and seminars on Divine Mercy. Most of these were given at the request of, or for, *The John Paul II Institute of Divine Mercy*, Stockbridge, MA, and/or *Life Foundation Ministries*, Bernalillo, NM.

In my discussions with the audience after speaking, I found many have not seriously read the Diary *("Too difficult and confusing.")*; many have attempted other books but found them to detailed or just filled with generalities.

When I would talk to priests and deacons more often than not they would say that they do not have time to go through all the different materials and put something together for their people. I would be the first to agree that their free time is very limited and the materials are scattered among too many books.

Finally, during my last series of talks during the 2008 Divine Mercy Sunday weekend in Phoenix, Arizona, my hosts were discussing this with me and said very simply: *"Why don't you just take your talks and put them in book form."* So I have.

This book is designed to be a single resource for priests, deacons, religious instructors and devotees of Divine Mercy.

Most books just quote a part of a sentence to give you the flavor of the idea presented. Then much time is lost in looking for the original source of the quotation. And your trend of thought is lost when, and if, you come back to that page. Also many people will not have the books or other sources that I will be quoting. Therefore, since it is to be a resource, I have insisted on certain criteria:

1. When giving a quote, I give the whole quote in context, so one does not have to go to the reference material (if they should have it) and spend valuable extra time searching and studying.
2. Facts and quotes are footnoted at the bottom of the page so that you do not have to keep flipping back and forth from the page you are reading to the footnote area; again coming back and losing you trend of thought.
3. Foreign words that are important to the topic are translated and in parenthesis I have placed the Latin, Greek and Hebrew texts and words.

It is my fond hope that this resource book will further an understanding of Divine Mercy and the essential devotionals associated with it and give more priests and deacons the impetus to expand the message and devotion.

When "Diary Entry" or "Diary" or "Diary Footnote" is written it refers to the book by Sister M. Faustina Kowalska, *Divine Mercy in My Soul, Diary,* (Stockbridge, MA: Marian Press) 1987.

Jesus' words in Diary quotes are in bold font to emphasize them.

Rio Rancho, New Mexico
December 12, 2009

Chapter 1
A Short Life Story of Saint Faustina

Introduction to Chapter 1
A Short Life Story of Saint Faustina

In preparation for the her canonization on April 30, 2000, I gave a weekend seminar on St. Faustina at the Convent of the Sisters of St. Francis of the Holy Eucharist in Independence, Missouri. I chose six topics, three of which are part of this book:

A Short Life Story of Saint Faustina (expanded in this chapter)

The Spiritual Life of Saint Faustina (expanded in Chapter 2)

The Image of Divine Mercy (greatly expanded in Chapter 5)

The obvious question is why I did not include a talk on the Chaplet of Divine Mercy at that seminar. The quick answer is that I had already presented a major talk on the Chaplet at The John Paul II Institute of Divine Mercy's *"An Ocean of Mercy"* Seminar in Houston in 1999. The expanded version is included as Chapter 4.

I believe this chapter, which is greatly expanded since 2000, gives the essence of St. Faustina's life that is necessary as background information without being overloaded with details.

A Short Life Story of Saint Faustina

In the early 1930's a young Polish nun by the name of Sr. Faustina Kowalska received extraordinary visions of Jesus Christ. He spoke to her of His abundant Mercy, His unlimited Mercy, and His "Ocean of Mercy" for all sinners and especially the greatest of sinners. And He offered His Mercy as a last hope of salvation before His Second Coming.

He taught her new prayers, a new prayer form, and a new devotion. Most importantly He taught her to have total abandonment (trust) to Him and His Mercy. That is the signature of Divine Mercy *"Jesus, I Trust in You"*. It is to be placed at the bottom of the Image of Divine Mercy. This is known as the heart of the Divine Mercy message and devotion.

For twenty years this devotion was suppressed by the Catholic Church because of mistranslations of her diary. A Cardinal of Poland, who believed in her message, had the diary reviewed and studied in detail by the Rev. Dr. Roziecki, STD, was resolved to submit it again to the Holy See. The restriction was lifted by Pope Paul VI in April of 1978. Six months after the Cardinal was successful with this effort, he, Karol Cardinal Wojtyla, was elected Pope.

The process to elevate Sr. M. Faustina to sainthood was begun in 1966 and on April 18, 1993 she was beatified, just four months after Pope John Paul II approved the first miracle. April 18, 1993, was the first Sunday after Easter, which Sunday is designation by Jesus to be the Feast of Divine Mercy. Sister Faustina's Feast is celebrated on October 5th, the date of her death.

On April 30, 2000, Pope John Paul II elevated Sister Faustina to Sainthood. April 30, 2000, is the First Sunday after Easter, the Sunday Jesus designated as the Feast of Divine Mercy. April 30, 1926, is the date Sr. Faustina received her habit and was given her religious name: Faustina.

Do not try to use Sr. Faustina's Diary as a biography. It is almost impossible. This will be explained in detail in Chapter 5, *The Image of Divine Mercy*.

There are several biographies available to read and study. First, *Sister Faustina Kowalska: Her Life and Mission,* by Maria Tarnawska; second, *Mercy, My Mission*, by Sister Sophia Michalenko, C.M.G.T.; and the one I recommend you read first is *Faustina, Apostle of Divine Mercy,* by Catherine M. Odell.

Sr. Faustina was born on August 25, 1905, the third child of Stanislaus and Marianna Kowalska. She was given the name Helena. Stanislaus was a carpenter and a farmer who lived near the village of Glogowiec, near Lodz, Poland. [1] Lodz is in the very center of present day Poland. Eventually Stanislaus and Marianna will have eight children.

The Kowalskis were poor country people and their life was very hard. In other times they would be called peasants or peons. Even though they were poor and their life hard, the Kowalskis were extremely happy and lived their faith every day. Helena was especially loved because she was the most joyful, obedient of their children, and she entertained her sisters and brothers with stories of the saints.

Most mothers who faithfully practice their faith and teach it to their children will tell you that children by nature are comfortable with the spiritual world. And they usually tend to be very contemplative.

From other people we learn that Helena had a very important dream around the age of five and shared it with her parents. She told them that the Blessed Mary had come to her, took her hand, and walked with her in a beautiful garden. Her parents did not know what to do with these dreams.

When her mother, Marianna, found her sitting up in bed at night and asked what she was doing, Helena responded that she thought her guardian angel was calling her to pray. [2]

We can presume that these experiences continued to increase and intensify, because it is Faustina herself who tells us something different took place around the age of 7. A phenomenon called inner locution [3] takes place.

---

1   Maria Tarnawska, *Sister Faustina Kowalska—Her Life and Mission* (Stockbridge, MA: Marian Helpers, 1989) p. 17

2   Sister Sophia Michalenko, C.M.G.T., *The Life of Faustina Kowalska* (Ann Arbor, MI, Servant Publications) 1999, p. 16

3   The word *locution* comes from the Latin *locutio,* a speaking, an utterance. Locutions are messages of diverse types and are received in differing manners. St. Teresa's division is simple: external, imaginary, intellectual. An *external locution* occurs from outside the person and is heard with one's bodily ears; one perceives that a human voice is speaking. The *imaginary locution* originates within the person, that is, within his inward sense faculties. The word *imaginary* does not mean here what it commonly signifies today: unreal, fabricated, illusory. It is simply an adjective referring to our inner sense capacity, the imagination, which enables us to recapture various sights,

"From the age of seven, I experienced the definite call of God, the grace of a vocation to the religious life. It was in the seventh year of my life that, for the first time, I heard God's voice in my soul; that is, an invitation to a more perfect life. But I was not always obedient to the call of grace. I came across no one who would have explained these things to me." [4]

It is from other sources that we will find that this experience took place during Vespers and the Exposition of the Blessed Sacrament in her parish church.

In 1914 Helena made her first communion. Because she had learned to read she met with her pastor several times a week to review her lessons. Actually it was very providential, since by the summer of 1915 the Lusitania

---

sounds, fragrances and the like through inner awareness of them. God can work directly within the faculty. *Intellectual locutions* occur in the deepest center of the person and with no sound, no voice. Yet they have remarkable traits. The intellectual enlightenment far surpasses anything of ordinary human study or experience. St Teresa tells us that

Once while with this presence of the three Persons that I carry about in my soul, I experienced so much light you couldn't doubt the living and true god was there. In this state He gave me understanding of things I didn't know how to speak of afterward. Among them was how the Person of the Son, and not the others, took flesh. (*Spiritual Testimony* 51)

She writes of another occasion:

While in prayer one day, I felt my soul to be so deep in God that it didn't seem there was a world, but while immersed in Him, understanding of that Magnificat verse, *et exultavit spiritus*, was given me in such a way I cannot forget it (*Spiritual Testimony* 56)

Understandably, most of what the saint has to say about locutions concerns the intellectual type… In the intellectual locution the words received are explicit, much more clear than those we hear with our bodily ears. One cannot resist listening to and understanding these words in the same way that one can choose to "turn off" mere human speech. When the Lord speaks in this manner, the recipient of the message listens whether wishing to or not. Understanding the words is likewise independent of one's will: when one wants to understand, one often cannot, when at other times one does not want to, one is made to understand. It is clear who the teacher is. CF. Thomas Dubay, S.M., *The Fire Within* (San Francisco, CA: Ignatius Press, 1989), p. 249.

4   Sister M. Faustina Kowalska, *Divine Mercy in My Soul, Diary,* (Stockbridge, MA: Marian Press) 1987, Diary Entry 7

had been sunk and regional military forces had drawn their front lines near Lodz.

Helena could not attend Church every Sunday since the family only had one good dress for the girls and they rotated wearing it. When she could attend she prayed for peace. And in early 1917 the Polish Patriot, Josef Pilsudski, was successful in establishing an independent Polish Republic.

Helena was enrolled in the Regional district School for the first time. Since she had been reading for several years, she was placed in the second grade. Her happiness in school didn't last long. She could already read. Therefore they decided that they needed the space for those who couldn't read. So after three terms, in the spring of 1919, she was asked to leave. Helena only received the equivalent of a second grade education. [5]

At the age of fifteen she asked her mother if she could work outside the house since her two older sisters already were doing that. With her mother's permission she left her poor village and went to work as a governess in well-to-do homes taking care of the children. She was a very happy and delightful young lady who pleased everyone for whom she worked.

She remained very devout in her Catholic faith. She continued to have mystical experiences and knew that Jesus was calling her to a more perfect life. Therefore, she left her housemaid and "governess" position for Mrs. Goryszewskis and returned home. [6] She asked her parents for permission to enter a convent. Her father refused to let her go because he could not supply the dowry needed to enter a religious order. Her response to her father that she didn't need money since Jesus Himself would lead her to a convent fell on deaf ears.

With permission she accepted several successive positions. When she was working as the governess for the Sadowska children she tried once more to be more comfortable with the world she had to live in. One night while at a dance with her sister in Lodz, she had the now famous vision of Jesus stripped of all His clothing, and covered with wounds. [7]

The following is a long quote, but she describes the situation in her own words:

> "Once I was at a dance [probably in Lodz] with one of my sisters. While everybody was having a good time, my soul was experiencing deep torments. As I began to dance, I suddenly saw Jesus at my side, Jesus racked with pain, stripped of His clothing, all covered with wounds, who spoke these words to me: **How long shall I put up with**

---

5   Michalenko, *op.cit.*, p. 19
6   *Ibid.*, p. 21.
7   *Ibid.*, pp, 21-24.

you and how long will you keep putting Me off? At that moment the charming music stopped, [and] the company I was with vanished from sight; there remained Jesus and I. I took a seat by my dear sister pretending to have a headache in order to cover up what took place in my soul. After a while I slipped out unnoticed, leaving my sister and all my companions behind and made my way to the Cathedral of Saint Stanislaus Kostka.

It was already beginning to grow light; there were only a few people in the cathedral. Paying no attention to what was happening around me, I fell prostrate before the Blessed Sacrament and begged the Lord to be good enough to give me to understand what I should do next.

10. Then I heard these words: **Go at once to Warsaw; you will enter a convent there.** I rose from prayer, came home, and took care of things that needed to be settled. As best I could, I confided to my sister what took place within my soul. I told her to say goodby to our parents, and thus, in my one dress, with no other belongings, arrived at Warsaw.

11. When I got off the train and saw that all were going their separate ways, I was overcome with fear. What am I to do? To whom should I turn, as I know no one? So I said to the Mother of God, "Mary, lead me, guide me." Immediately I heard these words within me telling me to leave the town and to go to a certain nearby village where I would find a safe lodging for the night. I did so and found in fact that everything was just as the Mother of God told me. Very early the next day, I rode back into the city and entered the first Church I saw [St. James Church at Grojecka Street in Ochota, a suburb of Warsaw]. There I began to pray to know further the will of God. Holy Masses were being celebrated one after another. During one of them I heard the words: **Go to that priest** [Father James Dabrowski, pastor of St. James' Parish] **and tell him everything; he will tell you what to do next.** After the Mass I went to the sacristy. (5) I told the priest all that had taken place in my soul, and I asked him to advise me where to take the veil, in which religious order.

13The priest was surprised at first, but told me to have strong confidence that God would provide for my future. "For the time being," he said, "I shall send you to a pious lady [Aldona Lipszycowa⁴] with whom you will stay until you enter a convent." When I called on this lady, she received me very kindly. During the time I stayed with her, I was looking for a convent, but at whatever convent door I knocked, I was turned away. Sorrow gripped my heart, and I said to the Lord Jesus, "Help me; don't leave me alone." At last I knocked on our door.⁵ (That is, the Congregation of the Sister of our Lady of Mercy.)

14. When Mother Superior, the present Mother General Michael[6] came out to meet me, she told me, after a short conversation, to go to the Lord of the house and ask whether He would accept me. I understood at once that I was to ask this of the Lord Jesus. With great joy, I went to the chapel and asked Jesus: "Lord of this house, do You accept me? This is how one of these sisters told me to put the question to You."

Immediately I heard this voice: **I do accept; you are in My Heart**. When I returned from the chapel, Mother Superior asked first of all, "Well, has the Lord accepted you?" I answered, "Yes." "If the Lord has accepted, [she said] then I also will accept."

15. This is how I was accepted. However, for many reasons I still had to remain in the world for more than a year with that pious woman [Aldona Lipszycowa], but I did not go back to my own home.

At that time I had to struggle with many difficulties, but God was lavish with His graces. An ever-greater longing for God began to take hold of me. The lady, pious as she was, did not understand the happiness of religious life and, in her kindheartedness began to make other plans for my future life. And yet, I sensed that I had a heart so big that nothing would be capable of filling it. And so I turned with all the longing of my soul to God." [8]

The superior writes in her memoirs that Faustina was *"no one special."* She tests Faustina by telling her that she is to go to work so she can pay for her wardrobe. In the summer of 1924 she begins work as a domestic and on August 1, 1925, almost 20, she applies again to the Congregation of the Sisters of Our Lady of Mercy and is accepted.

The Congregation of the Sisters of Our Lady of Mercy was formed in Laval, France, in 1818. The purpose of the congregation was to board, educate and reform young girls who fell into prostitution. The convent in Warsaw was founded in 1862. Helena was accepted as a "co-adjutor" in the order. This congregation had two groups of religious.

The first group, called "directresses," were well educated and were the teachers of the young women who were their "wards."

The sisters who were called "coadjutors" were in the second choir and did the housework for the community and offered up their prayers and work for the success of the ministry of the congregation. [9]

Helena knows virtually nothing about the congregation she joined; only

---

8   Diary Entries 9 to 15
9   Diary Footnote 61

that it was where she was led. With all the laundry and dishes to wash, and all the cooking to be done, she found that there is little time to pray.

But on or about August 22, 1925, she tells the Lord she wants to leave and go to a stricter order. That night He responds to her:

> "I came to my cell. The sisters were already in bed — the lights were out. I entered the cell full of anguish and discontent; I did not know what to do with myself. I threw myself headlong on the ground and began to pray fervently that I might come to know the will of God. There is silence everywhere as in the tabernacle. All the sisters are resting like white hosts enclosed in Jesus' chalice. It is only from my cell that God can hear the moaning of a soul. I did not know that one was not allowed to pray in the cell after nine without permission.
>
> After a while brightness filled my cell, and on the curtain I saw the very sorrowful Face of Jesus. There were open wounds on His Face, and large tears were falling on my bedspread. Not knowing what all this meant, I asked Jesus, "Jesus, who has hurt You so?" And Jesus said to me, **It is you who will cause Me this pain if you leave this convent. It is to this place that I called you and nowhere else; and I have prepared many graces for you.** I begged pardon of Jesus and immediately changed my decision.
>
> (7) The next day was confession day. I related all that had taken place in my soul, and the confessor answered that, from this, God's will is clear that I am to remain in this congregation and that I'm not even to think of another religious order. From that moment on, I have always felt happy and content." [10]

Shortly after this vision Sr. Faustina's sufferings begin.

> "Shortly after this, I fell ill [general exhaustion]. The dear Mother Superior sent me with two other sisters for a rest to Skolimow, not far from Warsaw. It was at that time that I asked the Lord who else I should pray for. Jesus said that on the following night He would let me know for whom I should pray.
>
> [The next night] I saw my Guardian Angel, who ordered me to follow him. In a moment I was in a misty place full of fire in which there was a great crowd of suffering souls. They were praying fervently, but to no avail, for themselves; only we can come to their aid. The flames which were burning them did not touch me at all. My Guardian Angel did not leave me for an instant. I asked these souls what their greatest

10   Diary Entry 19

suffering was. They answered me in one voice that their greatest torment was longing for God. I saw Our Lady visiting the souls in Purgatory. The souls call her "The Star of the Sea." She brings them refreshment. I wanted to talk with them some more, but my Guardian Angel beckoned me to leave. We went out of that prison of suffering. [I heard an interior voice] which said, **My mercy does not want this, but justice demands it**. Since that time, I am in closer communion with the suffering souls." [11]

This is probably the beginning of her suffering from tuberculosis brought on most likely by years of fasting and exhaustion from nightly vigils of prayer. All of these pious acts were without the benefit of good spiritual counsel or direction.

Helena is now a postulant, that is, one who is asking to enter the order. It is the first stage of the process for full acceptance. This is followed by the second stage, the *Novitiate*, which can be either one or two years. A novice is a member of the congregation, but just in a temporary way. After the Novitiate, if accepted to go on, the Novice is allowed to make temporary vows of Poverty, Chastity and Obedience. Years later they may be accepted into full commitment by making permanent vows.

In the spring of 1926, her group of postulants began to get ready for entering the Novitiate and receiving their habit for the first time. They are moved to Krakow and begin this process by making an eight-day retreat.

On April 30, 1926, each postulant processes to the altar in a white bridal gown symbolizing her marriage to Jesus Christ. They are given their religious names and their religious habits. They leave the Chapel, and quickly return dressed in their habits for the first time.

No one from her family attends the ceremony. It was not because they didn't want to attend, but because the letter of invitation arrived too late. [12]

The chronicles of the order and other memoirs tell us that she fainted while she waited in front of the altar to receive her habit. She fainted again when dressing in her habit. Those who saw this presumed she fainted because of nervousness or joy.

Helena was given the name Sister Mary Faustina. Faustina which means *fortunate, happy* or *blessed one"* is apparently the feminine form for the name of the Martyr Faustinus who was thrown in the Tiber River in 120 AD for refusing to sacrifice to the pagan gods.

It is prophetic for Helena that the name of a martyr was given to her.

---

11   Diary Entry 20
12   Tarnawska, *op.cit.*, p. 74-5.

On her habit day, her first day as a religious, she was told all that she would suffer:

> "The day I took the [religious] habit, God let me understand how much I was to suffer. I clearly saw to what I was committing myself. I experienced a moment of that suffering. But then God filled my soul again with great consolations." [13]

Later, in the Diary she will expand upon this name:

> "...I answered the Lord once again, "I am misery itself; how can I be a hostage [for others]?" **You do not understand this today. Tomorrow, during your adoration, I will make it known to you**. My heart trembled, as did my soul, so deeply did these words sink into my soul. The word of God is living.
>
> When I came to the adoration, I felt within my soul that I had entered the temple of the living God, whose majesty is great and incomprehensible. And He made known to me what even the purest spirits are in His sight. Although I saw nothing externally, God's presence pervaded me. At that very moment my intellect was strangely illumined. A vision passed before the eyes of my soul; it was like the vision Jesus had in the Garden of Olives. First, the physical sufferings and all the circumstances that would increase them; [then] the full scope of the spiritual sufferings and those that no one would know about. Everything entered into the vision: false suspicions, loss of good name. I've summarized it here, but this knowledge was already so clear that what I went through later on was in no way different from what I had known at that moment. My name is to be: 'sacrifice.'" [14]

She entered the Congregation of the Sisters of Our Lady of Mercy as a lay sister. Because she was a lay sister, uneducated, she could never go on to what *she* considered the full religious life. Her duties were that of cooking, cleaning and gardening.

The memories, writings and sworn testimonies of superiors, other sisters and people who knew her tell us that she was a well-balanced, humble, joyful and very obedient sister. She was amiable, and loved to talk and tell stories. She was nicknamed *"The lawyer"* because she liked to gesture with her hands

---

13 Diary Entry 22
14 Diary Entry 135

when she spoke. [15] But she was very ordinary! There was nothing that singled her out as someone of special quality or character.

Unknown to the other sisters and those who visited the convent, she was in physical, psychological and spiritual pain almost constantly. Undergoing tremendous spiritual development she was entering the *"dark night of the Soul,"* which began at the first year of her Novitiate, April 3, 1927 and ended before First Vows, April 16, 1928.

Although Sr. Faustina continued to receive visions that intensified during her postulancy and Novitiate she tells us that her mission of Divine Mercy and her association with the Divine Plan began on February 22, 1931. Let us put this in perspective. She will not take perpetual vows until May 1, 1933. She is still in temporary religious vows.

One night in her cell as she was praying alone she had a vision of Jesus. And she heard Jesus say, and this is from her Diary:

(18) + February 22, 1931
47. In the evening, when I was in my cell, I saw the Lord Jesus clothed in a white garment. One hand [was] raised in the gesture of blessing, the other was touching the garment at the breast. From beneath the garment, slightly drawn aside at the breast, there were emanating two large rays, one red, the other pale. In silence I kept my gaze fixed on the Lord; my soul was struck with awe, but also with great joy. After a while, Jesus said to me, **Paint an image according to the pattern you see, with the signature: 'Jesus, I trust in You.' I desire that this image be venerated, first in your chapel, and [then] throughout the world.**
48. **I promise that the soul that will venerate this image will not perish. I also promise victory over [its] enemies already here on earth, especially at the hour of death. I Myself will defend it as My own glory.'** [16]

At the same time, Jesus requested that a Feast of Mercy be celebrated in the entire Church as a sign of his unlimited love for mankind:

49 "When I told this to my confessor, [29] I received this for a reply: "That refers to your soul." He told me, "Certainly, paint God's image in your soul." When I came out of the confessional, I again heard words such as these: **My image already is in your soul. I desire that**

15   Catherine M. Odell, *Faustina: Apostle of Divine Mercy* (Our Sunday Visitor: Huntington, IN) 1998, p. 50
16   Diary Entries 47-48.

there be a Feast of Mercy. I want this image, which you will paint with a brush, to be solemnly blessed on the first Sunday after Easter; that Sunday is to be the Feast of Mercy." [17]

Now you can imagine how overawed this young woman is. She has little education to speak of. She is leading what appears to be an ordinary consecrated life as a second choir sister. She has not even taken perpetual vows. She is still in a time of trial and discernment with this congregation and she could be dismissed at anytime.

She has tried to tell her superiors and confessors about these things before. With trepidation she begins to tell her superiors and the other sisters about these visions again.

Consequently Sr. Faustina became a social outcast in her own order: the target of spiteful comments, whispers, sensational rumors and jokes among those around her.

I will quote several Diary Entries so that you will get an idea of the extent of these sufferings were. I begin with this:

"When I opened myself up to my superiors, one of them [probably Mother Michael or Mother Mary Joseph] understood my soul and the road God intended for me. When I followed her advice, I made quick progress towards perfection. But this did not last long. When I opened up my soul still more deeply, I did not obtain what I desired; it seemed to my superior that these graces [of which I was the object] were unlikely, and so I could not draw any further help from her. She told me it was impossible that God should commune with His creatures in such a way: "I fear for you, Sister; isn't this an illusion of some sort! (58) You'd better go and seek the advice of a priest." But the confessor did not understand me and said, "You'd better go, Sister, and talk about these matters with your superiors." And so I would go from the superiors to the confessor and from the confessor to the superiors, and I found no peace. These divine graces became a great suffering for me. And more than once I said to the Lord directly, "Jesus, I am afraid of You; could You not be some kind of a ghost?" Jesus always reassured me, but I still continued to be incredulous. It is a strange thing however: the more I became incredulous, the more Jesus gave me proofs that these things came from Him." [18]

Diary Entries 123 to 128 contain many important insights to her life in

---

17 Diary Entry 49
18 Diary Entry 122

the convent and I will cover most of these in Chapter 2, "The Spiritual Life of Sister Faustina." But let me quote only from this entry and then give a summary:

> 123. "+ When I saw that my mind was not being set at rest by my superiors, I decided to say nothing [to them] of these purely interior matters. Exteriorly I tried, as a good nun should, to tell everything to my superiors, but as for the needs of my soul, I spoke about these only in the confessional. For many very good reasons, I learned that a woman is not called to discern such mysteries. *I laid myself open to much unnecessary suffering.* For quite a long time I was regarded as one possessed by the evil spirit, and I was looked upon with pity, and the superior took certain precautionary actions in my respect. It reached my ears that the sisters also regarded me as such. And the sky grew dark around me. I began to shun these divine graces, but it was beyond my power to do so. Suddenly I would be enveloped in such recollection that, against my will, I was immersed in God, and the Lord kept me completely dependent upon Himself." [19]

She was like a child in expressing what she heard and saw. In her own words she "...*laid (herself) open to much unnecessary suffering.*" She was considered possessed, put on constant watch, looked upon either with pity as demented or scorn as spiritually presumptive. And with each criticism from the community or the priest confessors she would be tormented by Satan who told her that her "faithfulness and sincerity just brought her grief, pain and suffering. [20]

The author of the life of Sr. Faustina, Maria Tarnawska, sums up the nun's miserable life like this.

> "Sister Faustina, led by her Divine Master, now became used to living always in the shadow of His suffering. Her understanding of this greatest mystery of God's Mercy grew even deeper. She now understood that the essence of her intimacy with the Lord would depend on taking part in His Passion, and that it was precisely this that would be the core of her vocation." [21]

On May 1, 1933, Bishop Stanislaus Rospond placed a ring on Sr. Faustina's finger and she became a perpetually vowed Sister of Our Lady of Mercy. On May 25 she was sent to Vilnius to be the new gardener. This is approximately

---

19   *Ibid.*, 123
20   *Ibid.*, entry 123.1
21   Tarnawska, *op.cit.*, p. 140.

her 14th move. She was hoping this would be where she could settle into a permanent place of residence.

It is at Vilnius that she meets Fr. Michael Sopocko, the newly appointed convent confessor. Even though she knew that Jesus had selected this priest as her spiritual director (she had seen him twice in visions), her experience with confessors and spiritual directors made her cautious. Not only was he confessor to the convent, he was pastor of St. Michael's Church and a professor of theology at Stefan Batory University. Fr. Sopocko had been a chaplain in the army in World War I and spiritual director for the seminary of the Vilnius diocese.

As an experienced spiritual director he begins to test this sister with questions about the authenticity of her reports. She thought him to be superficial and perfunctory. So she sought another confessor. He decided to test her in the same manner. Boxed in, she decided to return to Fr. Sopocko.

By the fall Fr. Sopocko begins to believe in her, but decided to question her superiors and asked them to have Sr. Faustina given a complete physical and mental examination.

Then after New Year's 1934 at the direction of Fr. Sopocko she travels into Vilnius (accompanied by Mother Irene) to meet the artist, Eugene Kazimeriowski, a professor at the university. Each week she travels to meet with the artist to help direct the painting of the Image of Divine Mercy.

In June 1934, when Eugene Kazimeriowski completed it, Sr. Faustina was totally depressed. The Image did not come anywhere near to representing what she had seen when Jesus came to her. She was brooding over this and she told our Lord of her disappointment. He responded to her:

> "Once, when I was visiting the artist [Eugene Kazimeriowski] who was painting the image, and saw that it was not as beautiful as Jesus is, I felt very sad about it, but I hid this deep in my heart. When we had left the artist's house, Mother Superior [Irene] stayed in town to attend to some matters while I returned home alone. I went immediately to the chapel and wept a good deal. I said to the Lord, "Who will paint You as beautiful as You are?" Then I heard these words: **Not in the beauty of the color, nor of the brush lies the greatness of this image, but in My grace.**" [22]

Father Sopocko discovered that he couldn't respond quickly and properly to the multitude of messages that Sr. Faustina communicated to him verbally. So he asked that she begin to write these down. When asked by a member of

---

22   Diary Entry 313

the Congregation why Sr. Faustina was keeping a diary, Fr. Sopocko writes in his own memoirs how he answered that question:

"...I was a professor at the Seminary and at the School of Theology of the Stefan Batory University in Vilnius at the time. I had no time to listen to her lengthy confessions at the confessional, so I told her to write everything down and then to show it to me from time to time. This is how the Diary came into being. (Father Sopocko's letter of March 6, 1972). [23]

It is while she is under the spiritual direction of Fr. Michael Sopocko that the requests of Jesus begin to be fulfilled.

-Between January and June of 1934, the original Image of Divine Mercy is painted.

-In July 1934 she begins to write the Diary.

-In January 1935 Fr. Sopocko discusses the Feast of Divine Mercy with the Papal Nuncio, Archbishop Ciortesim in Rome.

-On Friday, April 26, 1935, Fr. Sopocko preaches a sermon on Divine Mercy which Sr. Faustina hears.

-On April 26-28, 1935, the Image is publicly displayed at the Ostra Brama on the First Sunday after Easter.

-In July 1937 the first holy cards with the Image of Divine Mercy are printed.

-In August 1937, Fr. Sopocko directs Sr. Faustina to commit the Novena to writing. (Received from Lord on Good Friday, 1937)
(Image and request for Feast Day received February 22, 1931)
(Chaplet prayers received September 13, 1935)

-Late 1937 the novena, the Chaplet and the Litany were published as a pamphlet under the name "Chrystus Krol Milosierdzia" "Christ, King of Mercy."

During this time her health deteriorates rapidly and she is moved from one convent to the next and one job to the next in order to aid her recovery. The moves keep her from direct communications with Fr. Sopocko. Her visions and mystical experiences intensify. She is becoming a victim soul for mercy. She has great periods of desolation, suffering and pain, but only short periods of consolation.

In September 1938, Fr. Sopocko visits her at the sanitarium in Pradnik and finds her is ecstasy. Later when she is taken from there back to the convent in Krakow on September 26, 1938, he visits her for the last time. He writes in his memoirs:

23   Diary Footnote 3

"She looked like an unearthly being…At that time I no longer had the slightest doubt that what she had written in her diary about receiving Holy Communion from an Angel was really true." [24]

Sr. Faustina's condition deteriorates rapidly and October 5, 1938, at 4 p.m., she makes her confession for the last time. The chaplain, Fr. Czaputa, with the sisters recites the prayers of the dying. Sr. Faustina, conscious to the end, joins in the prayers. At 10:45 PM she goes to the Lord for her reward.

On October 7, 1938, the Feast of Our Lady of the Rosary, after her funeral Mass, her body is buried in the cemetery next to the garden of the Congregation of the Sisters of Our Lady of Mercy in Krakow.

---

24   Tarnawska, *op.cit.*, p. 268

Chapter 2
The Spiritual Life of Saint Faustina

Introduction to Chapter 2
The Spiritual Life of Saint Faustina

As stated in the introduction to Chapter 1, this chapter was also part of a weekend Seminar given at the Convent of the Sisters of St. Francis of the Holy Eucharist in Independence, Missouri.

When writing on the spirituality of an individual it is very easy to get bogged down in minutiae. Although very important at times, it tends to detract from the overall understanding of the personal relationship the individual has with the Infinite.

When I studied for my Masters in Theology I chose my overall studies carefully, so that I would have a better understanding of the Spiritual Life.

I believe that St. Faustina's Diary gives an insight into her spiritual life that rivals St. Teresa of Avila and St. John of the Cross. The overall problem with the Diary is that fact that it does not follow a chronological order as normal diaries do. I explain this problem in this chapter and in chapters 5 & 6.

I believe that I have been able to give an overall understanding of St. Faustina's spiritual life that will assist anyone reading the Diary.

I personally hope that someday St. Faustina will be declared a Doctor of the Church.

The Spiritual Life of Saint Faustina

What is spirituality? What is the spiritual life?

In attempting to give a definition we must realize that its parameters must be defined by the teaching and tradition of the Catholic Church. Vatican II states:

> "The Catholic Church rejects nothing that is true and holy in these religions. She regards with sincere reverence those ways of conduct and of life, those precepts and teachings which, though differing in many aspects from the ones she holds and sets forth, nonetheless often reflect a ray of that Truth which enlightens all men. Indeed, she proclaims, and ever must pro-claim Christ "the way, the truth, and the life" (John 14:6), in whom men may find the fullness of religious life, in whom God has reconciled all things to Himself." [25]

Vatican II Council goes on to declare that there is only ONE spirituality for all members of the Church. It is defined thus:

> "22. The truth is that only in the mystery of the incarnate Word does the mystery of man take on light. Christ the Lord... fully reveals man to man himself and makes his supreme calling clear.... The Christian man, conformed to the likeness of that Son Who is the firstborn of many brothers, (27) received "the first-fruits of the Spirit" (Romans 8:23) by which he becomes capable of discharging the new law of love... Pressing upon the Christian to be sure, are the need and the duty to battle against evil through manifold tribulations and even to suffer death. But, linked with the paschal mystery and patterned

---

25   "Relation of the Church to Non-Christian Religions," Article 2

21

on the dying Christ, he will hasten forward to resurrection in the strength which comes from hope. (30) All this holds true not only for Christians, but for all men of good will in whose hearts grace works in an unseen way." [26]

During my master's courses in Spirituality I was drawn to two Dominicans, Reginald Garrigou-Lagrange, O.P. and John Arintero, O.P., whose books have been recently republished. They defended, restored, and created new interest in the traditional teachings that established the one path to Christian perfection called for by Vatican II: the path through ascetical and mystical stages of the Christian's life in Christ.

Without getting into theological differences of opinion as to what is *ascetical* and what is *mystical*, suffice it to say that our Christian Life is to follow the three stages of the interior life. The three stages are the *Purgative*, *Illuminative* and *Unitive*. A great treatise on this is by Fr. Reginald Garrigou-Lagrange: *The Three Ways of the Spiritual Life*.

Depending on the soul's practice of the evangelical counsels of poverty, chastity and obedience it passes through these as a preparation for and sustaining of its experiential knowledge of God.

This experiential knowledge of God comes through the infused graces of the theological virtues of faith, hope and love, and through the infused gift of prayer (generally under the title of contemplation). By "infused" is meant that you cannot acquire this gift on your own ability or initiative. It is only given by the will and action of God Himself.

This knowledge of God is sometimes accompanied by extraordinary phenomena: ecstasies, stigmata, bi-location, prophecy, ability to read the spiritual state of souls, etc.

Many people who are familiar with the Message and Devotion of Divine Mercy have little or no knowledge of Sr. Faustina's spiritual life. Most to whom I have talked know she was a pious religious who had extraordinary visitations from Jesus. Few who have read her diary in detail know that Sr. Faustina passed through all stages of the interior life and experienced not only ecstasies, visions, and locutions, but the passion of Jesus, the hidden stigmata, physical, psychological and spiritual torment from demons and Satan.

Sr. Faustina's Diary is the awe-inspiring journey of a soul through the mystical life. Her Diary is full of spiritual theological truths written by a poor peasant with limited education (only 2nd grade). Cardinal Andrew Deskur in the official introduction of the Polish Edition of the Diary (which is found in most English editions) writes:

---

26 "Pastoral Constitution on the Church in the Modern World," Article 22.

"...I am fully aware that I am introducing a document of Catholic mysticism of exceptional work, not only for the Church in Poland, but also for the universal Church." [27]

Later in the introduction he writes:

"...The theology alone which is found in the Diary awakens in the reader a conviction of its uniqueness; and if one considers the contrast between Sister Faustina's education and the loftiness of her theology, the contrast alone indicates the special influence of Divine Grace." [28]

We know that Helena at the age of 5 received a special dream which included the Blessed Mother holding her hand and strolling with her in a beautiful garden. [29]

She herself tells us in her Diary that God began to speak to her interiorly at the age of 7. [30] This is known as *inner locution*. [31] As she responded to this special call Helena began to make prayer vigils each night. She was being called more and more into a deeper prayer life.

What is most amazing is that she had virtually no spiritual guidance at this time. She herself recounts this in the same Diary Entry:

"...But I was not always obedient to the call of grace. I came across no one who would have explained these things to me." [32]

At first, for Sister Faustina, there are only locutions and bright lights:

"Satan's temptations during meditation. I felt a strange fear that the priest would not understand me, or that he would have no time to hear everything I would have to say. How am I going to tell him all this? If it were Father Bukowski I could do it more easily, but this Jesuit whom I am seeing for the first time.... Then I remembered Father Bukowski's advice that I should at least take brief notes of the lights sent to me by God during the retreats and give him at least a brief report on them..." [33]

---

27 Diary, p. xi
28 *Ibid.*, p. xii.
29 Michalenko, *op.cit.*, p. 16
30 Diary Entry 7
31 See Footnote 3 in Chapter 1.
32 Diary Entry 7
33 *Ibid.*,173

What is important is that on this occasion Sr. Faustina explains her doubts in the Diary and that she does not share them with her confessor. How blessed we should be to have a confessor as wise as she had. The Diary Entry continues:

"…My God, for a day and a half all has gone well, and now a life and death struggle is beginning. The conference is to start in a half-hour, and then I am to go to confession. Satan tried to persuade me into believing that if my superiors have told me that my inner life is an illusion, why should I ask again (87) and trouble the confessor? Didn't M.X. [probably Mother Jane] tell you that the Lord Jesus does not commune with souls as miserable as yours? This confessor is going to tell you the same thing. Why speak to him about all this? These are not sins, and Mother X. told you that all this communing with the Lord Jesus was daydreaming and pure hysteria. So why tell it to this confessor? You would do better to dismiss all this as illusions. Look how many humiliations you have suffered because of them, and how many more are still awaiting you, and all the sisters know that you are a hysteric. "Jesus!" I called out with all the strength of my soul." [34]

Notice she calls upon the name of Jesus. It is the Name each of us needs to scream during all our temptations.

The easiest pitfalls to fall into while trying to practice the spiritual life are scrupulosity and doubt, which lead to despair. Under the seal of confession Sr. Faustina gets beautiful advice.

But before I go into that, let me tell you what Jesus says to her about confession:

"Then I saw the Lord Jesus, as He is represented in the image, and He said to me, **Tell the confessor that this work is Mine and that I am using you as a lowly instrument.** And I said, "Jesus, I can no longer do anything You command me to do, because my confessor has told me that all this is an illusion, and that I am not allowed to obey any of Your commands. I will do nothing that You will tell me to do now. I am sorry, my Lord, but I am not allowed to do anything, and I must obey my confessor. Jesus, I most earnestly ask Your pardon. You know how much I suffer because of this, but it can't be helped, Jesus. The confessor has forbidden me to follow Your orders." Jesus listened to my arguments and complaints with kindness and satisfaction. I

---

34   *Ibid.*

thought (102) the Lord Jesus would be grievously offended but, on the contrary, He was pleased and said to me kindly, **Always tell your confessor about everything I say to you and command you to do, and do only that for which you obtain permission. Do not be upset, and fear nothing; I am with you.** My soul was filled with joy, and all those oppressive thoughts vanished. Certitude and courage entered my soul." [35]

To be obedient to her confessor is exactly the advice given to St. Teresa of Avila four hundred years before her.

Now let us return to when Sr. Faustina elects to tell the confessor only about the temptations from Satan and not the doubts.

"174 At the moment the priest came in and began the conference. He spoke for a short time, as if he were in a hurry. After the conference, he went over to the confessional. Seeing that none of the sisters were going there, I sprang from my kneeler, and in an instant was in the confessional. There was no time to deliberate. *Instead of telling the father about the doubts that had been sown in me in respect to my dealings with the Lord Jesus, I began to speak about these temptations I have just described above.* The confessor immediately understood my situation and said, "Sister, you distrust the Lord Jesus because He treats you so kindly. Well, Sister, be completely at peace. Jesus is your Master, and your communing with Him is neither daydreaming nor hysteria nor illusion. Know that you are on the right path. Please try to be faithful to these graces; you are not free to shun them. You do not need at all, Sister, *to tell your superiors about these interior graces, unless the Lord Jesus instructs you clearly to do so, and even then you should first consult with your confessor. But if the Lord Jesus demands something external, in this case, after consulting your confessor, you should carry out what He asks of you, even if this costs you greatly. On the other hand, you must tell your confessor everything. There is absolutely no other course for you to take, Sister. Pray that (88) you may find a spiritual director, or else you will waste these great gifts of God. I repeat once again, be at peace; you are following the right path.* Take no heed of anything else, but always be faithful to the Lord Jesus, no matter what anyone says about you. It is with just such miserable souls that the Lord Jesus communes in this intimate way. And the more you humble yourself, the more the Lord Jesus will unite Himself with you." [36]

35   *Ibid.*, Entry 645
36   *Ibid.*, Entry 174

Most of us can relate to Sr. Faustina's frustration at not having a good spiritual director. But in a sense we make our situation worse. Most of us do not even go to a regular confession in order to get spiritual guidance under the sacramental grace of Confession.

Notice the obedience of Sr. Faustina and the grace that resulted. She moves into one of the high points in spiritual life: to be able to interiorly sense the indwelling of the Trinity.

> "175 When I left the confessional, ineffable joy filled my soul, so that I withdrew to a secluded spot in the garden to hide myself from the sisters to allow my heart to pour itself out to God. God's presence penetrated me and, in an instant, all my nothingness was drowned in God; and at the same moment I felt, or rather discerned, the Three Divine Persons dwelling in me. And I had such great peace in my soul that I myself was surprised that I could have had so many misgivings.
> 176+ *Resolution:* Faithfulness to inner inspirations, even though I would have no idea how much I would have to pay for it. I must do nothing on my own without first consulting the confessor." [37]

Visions do come to Sr. Faustina. In fact, the first recorded one began when she is only 17. It is then that she has the famous vision of the suffering Jesus while she was in the dancehall in Lodz. [38] And these visions continue and intensify on and off throughout her life.

Most around her know she is very prayerful. But most do not know anything about her terrible sufferings and pain.

We know by hindsight that she must have been infected with tuberculosis at an early age. It is a disease very difficult to diagnose in its early stages. It can go virtually unnoticed in one who attempts rigorous fasting and deprivation of sleep in order to keep all night vigils of prayer.

Therefore, it happens that when she falls sick in exhaustion or because of illnesses she is often accused of being a malingerer or a fake. Diary Entries 122 through 128 speak of her sufferings from being misunderstood:

> "122. When I opened myself up to my superiors, one of them [probably Mother Michael or Mother Mary Joseph] understood my soul and the road God intended for me. When I followed her advice, I made quick progress towards perfection. But this did not last long. When I

37   *Ibid.*, Entry 175-6
38   *Ibid.*, Entry 9

opened up my soul still more deeply, I did not obtain what I desired; it seemed to my superior that these graces [of which I was the object] were unlikely, and so I could not draw any further help from her. She told me it was impossible that God should commune with His creatures in such a way: "I fear for you, Sister; isn't this an illusion of some sort! (58) You'd better go and seek the advice of a priest. " But the confessor did not understand me and said, "You'd better go, Sister, and talk about these matters with your superiors." And so I would go from the superiors to the confessor and from the confessor to the superiors, and I found no peace. These divine graces became a great suffering for me. And more than once I said to the Lord directly, "Jesus, I am afraid of You; could You not be some kind of a ghost?" Jesus always reassured me, but I still continued to be incredulous. It is a strange thing however: the more I became incredulous, the more Jesus gave me proofs that these things came from Him." [39]

Notice the conflict created by her obedience. She is being sent by the priest to the superior. Then the superior sends her to the priest. It is a spiritual run around.

"123+ When I saw that my mind was not being set at rest by my superiors, I decided to say nothing [to them] of these purely interior matters. Exteriorly I tried, as a good nun should, to tell everything to my superiors, but as for the needs of my soul, I spoke about these only in the confessional. For many very good reasons, I learned that a woman is not called to discern such mysteries. *I laid myself open to much unnecessary* suffering. For quite a long time I was regarded as one possessed by the evil spirit, and I was looked upon with pity, and the superior took certain precautionary actions in my respect. It reached my ears that the sisters also regarded me as such. And the sky grew dark around me. I began to shun these divine graces, but it was beyond my power to do so. *Suddenly I would be enveloped in such recollection that, against my will, I was immersed in God, and the Lord kept me completely dependent upon Himself.*" [40]

Notice this sentence:

"Suddenly I would be enveloped in such recollection that, against

---

39   *Ibid.*, Entry 122
40   *Ibid.*, Entry 123

my will, I was immersed in God, and the Lord kept me completely dependent upon Himself."

When a soul surrenders totally to God, God takes the soul at its word. God takes over; many times to the embarrassment of the soul. Remember St. John of Cupertino? He was embarrassed when he was caused to levitate in public.

Continuing Sr. Faustina wrote:

124.   *"In the initial moments my soul is always a little frightened, but later it is filled* with a strange peace and strength."

125.   "All these things could still be endured. But when the Lord demanded that I should paint that picture, they began to speak openly about me and to regard me as a hysteric and a fantasist, and the rumors began to grow louder. One of the sisters came to talk to me in private. She began by pitying me and said, "I've heard them say that you are a *fantasist*, Sister, and that you've been having visions. My poor Sister, defend yourself in this matter." (59) She was a sincere soul, and she told me sincerely what she had heard. But I had to listen to such things every day. God only knows how tiring it was." [41]

What is a fantasist?

A fantasist is one who is a visionary or dreamer. On the negative side a fantasist is a boaster, one who is ostentatious. One can understand how some of the sisters would get that impression. Here we have an uneducated poor sister of the 2nd choir saying Jesus is demanding this or that. What is real and what is illusionary? What is true and what is the result of a fantastic imagination? Faced with this, Sr. Faustina takes the action most prudent persons would take. She chooses to remain silent.

"Yet, I resolved to bear everything in silence and to give no explanations when I was questioned. Some were irritated by my silence, especially those who were more curious. Others, who reflected more deeply, said, "Sister Faustina must be very close to God if she has the strength to bear so much suffering." *It was as if I were facing two groups of judges. I strove after interior and exterior silence.* I said nothing about myself, even though I was questioned directly by some sisters. My lips were sealed. I suffered like a dove, without complaint. But some sisters seemed to find pleasure in vexing me in whatever way they could. My

---

41   *Ibid.*, Entries 124-5

patience irritated them. But God gave me so much inner strength that I endured it calmly." [42]

Have you ever had the experience of trying to please one group only to have the other group jump into your business and complain? When you ignore both, you are caught in the crossfire? She was.

"I learned that I would have help from no one at such moments, and I started to pray and beg the Lord for a confessor. My only desire was that some priest would say this one word to me, "Be at peace, you are on the right road," or "Reject all this for it does not come from God." But I could not find such a priest who was sufficiently sure of himself to give me a definite opinion in the name of the Lord. And so the uncertainty continued. O Jesus, if it is Your will that I live in such uncertainty, may Your Name be blessed! *I beg You, Lord, direct my soul yourself and be with me, for of myself I am nothing.*" [43]

Jesus will answer this prayer. He wants her to be totally dependent upon Him. And that means suffering through the unexplainable.

"Thus I have already been judged from all sides. There is no longer anything in me that has escaped the sisters' judgment. But it seems now to have worn itself out, and they have begun to leave me in peace. *My tormented soul has had some rest, and I have learned that the Lord has been closest to me in times of such persecutions. This [truce] lasted for only a short time.* A violent storm broke out again. And now the old suspicions became, for them, as if true facts, and once again I had to listen to the same old songs. The Lord would have it that way. But then, strangely enough, even exteriorly I began to experience (60) various failure. This brought down on me many sufferings of all sorts, known to God alone..." [44]

But notice her statement *"My tormented soul has had some sort of rest, and I have learned that the Lord has been closest to me in times of such persecutions. This [truce] lasted for only a short time."* Her consolations were very short when they did come. They do not seem to match the intensity or duration of her suffering.

---

42   *Ibid.*, Entry 126
43   *Ibid.*, Entry 127
44   *Ibid.*, Entry 128

There is a key to a true spiritual life in the last line of the above quoted entry.

> "This brought down on me many sufferings of all sorts, known to God alone."

This total abandonment caused great pain since it magnified the intensity of the rejection she felt from the Trinity: just as Jesus said on the Cross: *"Eli Eli Lama Sabachtani?" "My God, My God, why have you abandoned me?"* [45]

One of my spirituality teachers talking about *Suffering with Christ* used a phrase that is most apropos here: *"To follow Jesus in Abandonment is TO LIVE ALONE and TO DIE UNKNOWN."* [46]

As long as Sr. Faustina lived on this earth, she would be misunderstood and her spiritual life virtually unknown to others. However, her death will make her shine like a star, because she is a great teacher of the spiritual life for the growth of the Church. She is one of those Daniel speaks about:

> "Those who are wise will shine as brightly as the expanse of the heavens, and those who have instructed many in uprightness, as bright as stars for all eternity." [47]

How would you like to strive earnestly to do what Jesus wanted you to do, you pray, but every time you turned around you find you were being spied upon, even when you tried to get needed rest? The Diary continues:

> "...But I tried as best I could to do everything with the purest of intentions. I could now see that everywhere I was being watched like a thief: in the chapel; while I was carrying out my duties; in my cell.[40] I was now aware that, besides the presence of God, I had always close to me a human presence as well. And I must say that, more than once, this human presence bothered me greatly. There were times when I wondered whether I should undress to wash myself or not. Indeed, even that poor bed of mine was checked many times.[41] More than once I was seized with laughter when I learned they would not even leave my bed alone. One of the sisters herself told me that came she to observe me in my cell every evening to see how I behave in it.

Still, superiors are always superiors. And although they humiliated

---

45   Matthew 27: 46
46   Author unknown.
47   Daniel 12: 3

me personally and, on occasions, filled me with all kinds of doubts, they always allowed me to do what the Lord demanded. Though not in the way I asked, but in some other way, they fulfilled the Lord's demands and gave me permission for all the rigors and mortifications [He asked of me].

One day, one of the Mothers [probably Mother Jane] poured out so much of her anger on me and humiliated me so much that I thought I would not be able to endure it. She said to me, "You queer, hysterical visionary, get out of this room; go on with you, Sister!" She continued to pour out upon my head everything she could think of. When I got to my cell, I fell on my face before the cross, and then looked at Jesus; but I could no longer say a single word. Yet I concealed everything from the others and pretended that nothing had happened between us." [48]

Some people have said to me that they could take the sufferings Sr. Faustina had to endure if they had the consolations that she received. I don't think so. Read her comments about her sufferings:

"I do not know how to describe all that I suffer, and what I have written thus far is merely a drop. There are moments of suffering about which I really cannot write. But there are also moments in my life when my lips are silent, and there are no words for my defense, and I submit myself completely to the will of God; then the Lord Himself defends me and makes claims on my behalf, and His demands are such that they can be noticed exteriorly. Nevertheless, when I perceive His major interventions, which manifest themselves by way of punishment, then I beg Him earnestly for mercy and forgiveness. Yet I am not always heard. The Lord acts toward me in a mysterious manner. There are times when He Himself allows terrible sufferings, and then again there are times when He does not let me suffer and removes everything (44) that might afflict my soul. These are His ways, unfathomable and incomprehensible to us. It is for us to submit ourselves completely to His holy will. There are mysteries that the human mind will never fathom here on earth; eternity will reveal them." [49]

This is one of the things that remains a mystery. When you become close to Jesus Christ and He becomes your intimate lover and you have a

---

48   Diary Entry 128
49   *Ibid.*, Entry 1656

love relationship with Him, Jesus like every lover wants to share the most intimate triumphs and sufferings with His beloved. Sr. Faustina wrote to Sister Ludwina:

> "The bride must resemble her Betrothed, namely through sacrifice and self-immolation. She should faithfully follow in His footsteps and not be afraid of anything, because love is measured by the degree of sacrifice and suffering." [50]

The greatest glory that Jesus Christ can give to anyone that loves Him is the possibility of participating in His passion and death. And so it is that we have people who are called to the experience of the mystical marriage. They experience the Passion of Jesus and may receive the stigmata.

After her recounting of all these sufferings Sister Faustina tells us the good of abandoning oneself to Christ completely. She does so herself and Jesus accepts her offer. The Way of Cross and the Passion of Jesus Christ become the way of the rest of Sr. Faustina's Life:

> "134 (63) + O my Jesus, You have tested me so many times in this short life of mine! I have come to understand so many things, and even such that now amaze me. Oh, how good it is to abandon oneself totally to God and to give Him full freedom to act in one's soul!

> 135 During the third probation, the Lord gave me to understand that I should offer myself to Him so that He could do with me as He pleased. I was to remain standing before Him as a victim offering. At first, I was quite frightened, as I felt myself to be so utterly miserable and knew very well that this was the case. I answered the Lord once again, "I am misery itself; how can I be a hostage [for others]?" **You do not understand this today. Tomorrow, during your adoration, I will make it known to you.** My heart trembled, as did my soul, so deeply did these words sink into my soul. The word of God is living. When I came to the adoration, I felt within my soul that I had entered the temple of the living God, whose majesty is great and incomprehensible. And He made known to me what even the purest spirits are in His sight. Although I saw nothing externally, God's presence pervaded me. At that very moment my intellect was strangely illumined. A vision passed before the eyes of my soul; it was like the vision Jesus had in the Garden of Olives. First, the physical sufferings

---

50   *The Letters of Saint Faustina,* translated by Sr. M. Beata Piekut O.L.M., (Cracow, Poland, Misericordia Publications) 2007, p. 157.

and all the circumstances that would increase them; [then] the full scope of the spiritual sufferings and those that no one would know about. Everything entered into the vision: false suspicions, loss of good name. I've summarized it here, but this knowledge was already so clear that what I went through later on was in no way different from what I had known at that moment. *My name is to be: "sacrifice.*

When the vision ended, a cold sweat bathed my forehead. Jesus made it known to me that, even if I did not give my consent to this, I could still be saved; and He would not lessen His graces, but would still continue to have the same intimate relationship with me, so that even if I did not consent to make this sacrifice, God's generosity would not lessen thereby." [51]

But St. Faustina reiterates that it must be by your free consent to abandon your will to His:

"And the Lord gave me to know that the whole mystery depended on me, on my free consent to the sacrifice given with full use of my faculties. In this free and conscious act lies the whole power and value before His Majesty. Even if none of these things for which I offered myself would ever happen to me, before the Lord everything was as though it had already been (64) consummated.

At that moment, I realized I was entering into communion with the incomprehensible Majesty. I felt that God was waiting for my word, for my consent. Then my spirit immersed itself in the Lord, and I said, "Do with me as You please. I subject myself to Your will. As of today, Your holy will shall be my nourishment, and I will be faithful to Your commands with the help of Your grace. Do with me as You please. I beg You, O Lord, be with me at every moment of my life." [52]

Sister Faustina became a "Victim Soul." A victim soul is one who has been asked by Jesus to participate in His sufferings and to help Him gain souls through those sufferings. There are two scripture statements that support this.

Saint Paul tells us:

---

51   Diary, Entries 134 and 135
52   *Ibid.*, Entry 136

"And Yet I am alive; yet it is no longer I, but Christ Living in me." [53]

After this Saint Paul states:

"After this let no one trouble me: I carry branded on my body the marks of Jesus." [54]

Saint Paul also suffered as a victim soul for Jesus since he tells us in Colossians:

"It makes me happy to be suffering for you now, and in my own body to make up all the hardships that still have to be undergone by Christ for the sake of his body, the Church." [55]

Faustina alludes to Saint Paul's saying in her Diary:

"At the same time, I saw a certain person [Father Sopocko] and, in part, the condition of his soul and the ordeals God was sending him. His sufferings were of the mind and in a form so acute that pitied him and said to the Lord, "Why do you treat him like that?" And the Lord answered, **For The sake of his triple crown.** And the Lord also gave me to understand what unimaginable glory awaits the person who resembles the (67) suffering Jesus here on earth. That person will resemble Jesus in His glory. The Heavenly Father will recognize and glorify our soul to the extent that He sees in us a resemblance to His Son. I understood that this assimilation into Jesus is granted to us while we are here on earth. I see pure and innocent souls upon whom God has exercised His justice; these souls are the victims who sustain the world and who fill up what is lacking in the Passion of Jesus. They are not many in number. I rejoice greatly that God has allowed me to know such souls." [56]

In 1933, shortly after Sr. Faustina made her perpetual vows she met two priests who put order and happiness into her chaotic life. First, she spoke to a new confessor whose authoritative comforting words removed the majority of doubts that were haunting her when he said:

---

53 Galatians 2: 20
54 *Ibid.*, 6: 17
55 Colossians 1: 24
56 Diary, Entry 604

"...Sister be completely at peace..." [57]

She later recorded him as saying in the same Entry:

"...Jesus is your master and you communing with Him is neither daydreaming nor hysteria, nor illusion. Know that you are on the right path... There is absolutely no other course for you to take. Pray that you might find a spiritual director or else you will waste these great gifts of God..."

Then weeks later all of Sr. Faustina's doubts left after she met the priest Michael Sopocko. She already felt that she knew him because Jesus had given her two visions of Fr. Sopocko, since he was to become her spiritual director. [58]

Fr. Sopocko was highly educated in pastoral and moral theology and perfectly suited for the job which he accepted readily. In the beginning she thought Father didn't fully believe in the authenticity of his new confidant's relationship with Jesus. Once Fr. Sopocko did accept her unique relationship with Jesus, he joined her efforts in proclaiming the message of Divine Mercy.

These are two very important lessons for us to learn from her life.

NUMBER ONE, you need a spiritual director like St. Theresa of Avila said.

"I have consulted many learned men because for some years now, on account of a greater necessity, I have sought them out more; and I've always been a friend of men of learning. For though some don't have experience, they don't despise the Spirit nor do they ignore it, because in Sacred Scripture, which they study, they always find the truth of the good spirit." [59]

And NUMBER TWO, even though Father Sopocko came to understand that he was called by Jesus to help her, he still discerned everything. We must remember that we never take anything at face value as Christians. We are told

---

57   *Ibid.*, Entry 174

58   You can find these in Diary Entries 53 and 61

59   St. Teresa of Avila, "The Life," from *The Collected Works of St. Teresa*, volume 1, translated by Kieran Kavanaugh and Otilio Rodriguez (copyright 1976 by Washington Province of Discalced Carmelites. ICS Publications, 2131 Lincoln Road NE, Washington D.C. 20002), no. 18, page 95.

by St. John to test all spirits. [60] Always test them. Remember St. Bernadette of Soubirous throwing holy water at the Blessed Mother? What did Mary do?

> "There she is!' she said suddenly during the second decade of the rosary. Marie, one of the girls with her, handed her a vial of holy water. Louise Soubirous had been afraid that something evil was showing itself at Massabielle. The holy water was insurance. 'But the more I sprinkled, the more she smiled, and I kept sprinkling until the bottle was empty.' The girl later told others. [61]

In The Diary of Sister Faustina we have the messages that were written in the last four years of her life. Most people don't know that when she was about half way through writing the messages the devil appeared to her as an angel of light and told her to burn the diary as trash! And what did she do? She burnt her diary. We find this in The Diary:

> "That is elsewhere in the diary. For a long time Sister Faustina did not take notes of her experiences and of graces received. It was only at the explicit order of her confessor, Father Sopocko, that she began to write down her experiences as they occurred, and also earlier ones as she remembered them. After some time, she burned her notes. Father Sopocko gives the following account: "When I was in the Holy Land for a few weeks, she was persuaded by a supposed angel to burn the diary. As penance, I told her to reconstruct the part destroyed. But in the meantime new experiences came, and she wrote down new and old things alternately. Hence the lack of chronological order in the diary." [62]

Discernment! Discernment! Even the saints have a problem with this. As a result she had to start all over again.

The pages of her handwritten journal penned from 1934 to 1938 turned into nearly 700 printed pages, which were published as the *Diary, Divine Mercy in My Soul* by Sister M. Faustina Kowalska. It reveals her thoughts, her prayers, and day to day relationship with Jesus as well as the entire Divine Mercy message from Jesus.

Some theologians believe the writings to be as spiritually insightful as those of St. Theresa of Avila and St. Catherine of Siena, two Doctors of the

---

60   I John 4: 1-3
61   Catherine M. Odell, *Those Who Saw Her,* (Huntington, IN: Our Sunday Visitor Publishing Division, 1995) p. 92.
62   Diary, Footnote 42

Church. Just recently St. Theresa of Lisieux was elevated by the late Pope John Paul II as a Doctor of the Church. She is now the third (woman) Doctor of the Church.

It is my earnest prayer that soon Saint Faustina will be acknowledged as a Doctor of the Church.

Chapter 3
What is Mercy?

Introduction to Chapter 3
What is Mercy?

When I received the invitation to participate in some Divine Mercy talks on Catholic Family Radio, I didn't hesitate to accept. I was asked to give this introductory talk on the meaning of the word *Mercy*.

I searched my personal library for books on Mercy or books that even remotely talked about mercy. Besides the *Diary of Sister Faustina*, I found three books: One by Father George Kosicki, C.S.B., *Trust and Mercy*, one by Father George Maloney, S.J., *God's Incredible Mercy*, and one by Kenneth Copeland *The Mercy of God*. Since I had already read these books I began an intense review of each. Each is excellent in its own way. But I didn't find the catalyst to begin my talk.

So I went seeking more books in the library of the local Catholic College. There I did not find one book with Mercy in the title! Then I began a search through the reference volumes listing all the books in print. Amazing! The books I found could be counted on the fingers of one hand.

Now I understood Father George Maloney's feelings when he wrote this passage in the Introduction to his book, *God's Incredible Mercy:*

> "When I first thought of writing a book on God's mercy, I checked the libraries of several Catholic universities, all of which offered master and doctoral degrees in theology. To my surprise I was unable to find a single title on God's mercy. There were books on God's love. One library had a book dealing with the corporal and spiritual works of mercy that we are supposed to carry out. But not one book on God's mercy" [63]

---

63 Maloney, S.J., George A., *God's Incredible Mercy* (Alba House, New York,

What was to be a simple task of presenting old material in a new way turned into a frustrating situation similar to trying to start a fire without a spark.

Even though the series on Divine Mercy did not air, I did present my paper during the John Paul II Institute of Divine Mercy's *"Divine Mercy On-Site Seminar"* in Poland and Lithuania in 2001. My wife, Penny, and I were presenters during the seminar.

I decided because of all the difficulty I had in finding information on *"What is Mercy"* and how well the topic had been received at the seminar, it would be appropriate to expand my study of the subject for those who need the information as background for talks and sermons. This is the end product.

1989), pp. xi-xii.

What is Mercy?

What is Mercy?

As I asked the question over and over I did what I do in every situation, especially difficult ones. I called upon the Lord's help. Immediately, this scripture from the Gospel of Matthew came to mind:

> "Well then, every scribe who becomes a disciple of the Kingdom of heaven is like a householder who brings out from his storeroom new things as well as old." [64]

In my experience in teaching scripture I have found that sometimes you need to begin not with scripture itself, but with something with which the audience might be more familiar.

There are two things from non-scripture sources covering the word mercy with which I would like to begin.

The *first* is a story whose source I have long forgotten.

> "It seems there was a young man who had attempted to kill Emperor Napoleon. Because of the nature of the assassination attempt the Emperor elected to have a public display of the execution of the man. When all were assembled in the plaza and the execution about to begin, the mother of the accused young man came running up the steps of the platform where Napoleon sat, evading all the guards. She thrown herself at Napoleon's feet and wept bitterly begging for her son's pardon. Napoleon was heard to say: 'Madam, your son does not deserve pardon.' To which she answered: 'That is why they call it mercy.'"

---

64   Matthew 13: 52

My *second* source most people will recognize as the great courtroom speech given by Portia in the *Merchant of Venice*. In it Shakespeare eloquently cites the qualities of divine and human Mercy:

"The quality of mercy is not strain'd
It droppeth as the gentle rain from heaven
Upon the place beneath; it is twice blest;
It blesseth him that gives, and him that takes;
Tis mightiest in the mightiest; it becomes
The throned monarch better than his crown;
His Sceptre shows the force of temporal power,
The attribute to awe and majesty,
Wherein doth sit the fear and dread of Kings;
But mercy is above this sceptred sway;
It is enthroned in the hearts of Kings;
It is an attribute to God Himself;
And earthly power doth then show likest God's
When mercy seasons justice. Therefore, Jew,
Though justice be thy plea, consider this,
That, in the course of justice, none of us
Should see salvation: we do pray for mercy;
And that same prayer doth teach us all to render
The deeds of mercy." [65]

What powerful poetry! Now let us focus on these lines:

"Therefore, Jew, though justice be thy plea, consider this, that, in the course of justice, none of us should see salvation: we do pray for mercy;"

Let me narrow it down a little bit more:

"...in the course of justice, none of us should see salvation..."

Shakespeare has Portia saying to Shylock that if we were subject to justice only, we would never see salvation. That is why we pray for mercy.

These two citations, the story about Napoleon and the quotation from the *Merchant of Venice*, show us that mercy stays or holds back and delays the hand of justice. What happens after that is the unexpected.

---

65   Shakespeare, William, *The Merchant of Venice*, Act 4, Scene 1.

St. Thomas Aquinas makes this point in his *Summa Theologiae*:

> "Again, mercy is a relaxing of justice. However, God can not leave undone what his justice demands." [66]

Ever since our father and mother, Adam and Eve, sinned in the Garden of Eden by disobeying God, God has dealt with man at a distance. This distance between God and Man was not in God's original plan. Adam and Eve were created so that God could walk with them in the cool of the evening. [67]

Any lawyer or judge will tell you that a law that has no sanctions is not realistic, and points to the imprudence of the lawgiver. Obviously, God is not imprudent.

God explicitly stated that there were consequences and punishment for disobedience as He gave the command to Adam and Eve:

> "Then Yahweh God gave the man this command, 'You are free to eat of all the trees in the garden. But of the tree of the knowledge of good and evil you are not to eat; for, the day you eat of that, you are doomed to die." [68]

Death is the consequence of this sin of disobedience. Thus this first sin (the original sin [69]) of our parents, Adam and Eve, resulted in their and our loss of temporal and eternal life. Paul tells us:

> "Well, then, it was through one man that sin came into the world, and through sin death, and thus death has spread through the whole human race because everyone has sinned." [70]

---

66   Aquinas, St. Thomas, *Summa Theologiae*, (Image Books, Garden City, New York, 1969), 1A., q. 21, 3 (2), (Volume 2, p.144)

67   Genesis 3: 8

68   Genesis 2: 16-17

69   Original Sin: *The Council of Trent* (session 5, Cannons 1-5) in 1546 defined the doctrine as follows: 1) *"The whole of Adam, body and soul,"* lost, both for himself and his descendants, original *"justice and holiness,"* and *"incurred death"* and *"God's anger,"* plus *"bondage"* to *"the devil."* 2) This sin is passed on *"by propagation,"* and its sinful nature and guilt (though not all its consequences) can be blotted out only through Christ in Baptism. 3) *"Concupiscence (lust or "a tendency to sin") remains in the baptized,"* but it cannot morally *"harm those who do not consent"* and, by Jesus' grace, *"manfully resist."* Our Sunday Visitor's Encyclopedia of Catholic Doctrine, Russell Shaw, editor (Our Sunday Visitor, Huntington, IN, 1997) p. 482.

70   Romans 5: 12

Adam and Eve's disobedience resulted not only in the loss of their original state of holiness and righteousness before God, but also for all human beings. After the first sin, this world was virtually inundated by the consequences of sin, which is more evil. Just look around, we live in a world overwhelmed and permeated with the shame of abuse, murder, war, pain, hatred, illicit sex, depression, drugs, lying, cheating, stealing, manipulation and the culture of death. St. Paul expresses this very well when he writes:

> "It was not for its own purposes that creation had frustration imposed on it, but of the purposes of him who imposed it—with the intention that the whole creation itself might be freed from its slavery to corruption and brought into the same glorious freedom as the children of God. We are well aware that the whole creation, until this time, has been groaning in labour pains." [71]

God abhors sin! Because of the disobedience and sin of Adam, God's justice demands the death of the man. However, Adam doesn't die immediately – physically, that is. This indicates that something else is at work. God threatens death, but death seems to be delayed. What are the punishments that are immediately meted out?

> "To the woman he said: I shall give you intense pain in childbearing, You will give birth to your children in pain. Your yearning will be for your husband, And he will dominate you. "To the man he said, 'Because you listened to the voice of your wife and ate from the tree of which I had forbidden you to eat, Accursed be the soil because of you! Painfully will you get your food from it as long as you live. [18] It will yield you brambles and thistles, as you eat the produce of the land. [19] By the sweat of your face will you earn your food, until you return to the ground, as you were taken from it. For dust you are and to dust you shall return.'" [72]

Banishment, labor pains, domination, hard work, sweat and returning to dust, seem minor compared to the threaten punishment of immediate death. Since God as the lawgiver cannot be imprudent, do we not rightly draw the conclusion that something else is working here? That something else we find out is God's mercy.

While the book of Genesis tells us that in sorting out the responsibilities

---

71   Romans 8: 20-22
72   Genesis 3: 16-19

for this sin, God exacts what appears to be a lesser retribution, it also tells us that God gives a prophetic hint of recovery and reconciliation through the woman's offspring:

> "I shall put enmity between you and the woman, and between your offspring and hers; it will bruise your head and you will strike its heel." [73]

If we look to our secular law we begin to understand what is going on and what is not going on here. In secular law we find that an offense is measured from *two* aspects.

First, an offense is measured from the aspect of the nature of the offense committed by the perpetrator. For example, depending on the person's state of mind and other circumstances, the taking of the life of another person might be a premeditated murder, an accidental homicide, or a freak accident.

Second, an offense is measured from the aspect of the person against whom the crime is committed. The taking of the life might be strictly a murder. However, the dignity of the person or the office which the *victim* holds might elevate a simple taking of life or murder to a higher degree.

For example, because of the dignity of his office, the taking of the life of the President of the United States is not simple murder, it is an assassination. Therefore, the punishment or retribution must be in accordance with the dignity of the person offended. To insure that the punishment meets the crime, this crime is a federal, not a state, crime. And the punishment demanded is the death penalty.

It follows reasonably that an offense against God is an *infinite* evil because of the *infinite* dignity of God! Therefore, the retribution demanded is an *infinite* retribution.

Which in the case of the sin of our first parents, the *infinite retribution* should be the withdrawal of life. Life is the essence of God. God gives His name as Yahweh: *I AM HE WHO IS.* [74] In a sense we could say, God does not exist! He *is* existence. If there is no immediate withdrawal of life, there still must be a compensation of infinite worth to offset the infinite offense.

But Man being *finite* is incapable of performing *infinite* retribution! Therefore, from a justice point of view, Life should be withdrawn from man forever because there will be no infinite expiation performed by finite man.

Expiation of the sentence imposed by God must be made by a Man who is capable of performing *infinite* works. That demands a God/Man: one who is both infinitely God and finitely Man. Here begins our understanding of

---

73　Genesis 3: 15
74　Exodus 3: 14

Redemption and Salvation History referred to as Vicarious Expiation. Fr. John Hardon, S.J. in a conference he gave to the Institute of Religious Life stated:

> "More profoundly, however, Christ underwent the limitations of human nature as a means of meriting our salvation. Behind His experience of our weakness stands the idea of *vicarious expiation*. Injustice can be undone by justice, evil by goodness, whether of the man who did wrong or, of a friend who pays in his stead. As Thomas puts it: "Fairness demands that a man who owes a debt because of his wrongdoing should be set free on paying the penalty. What our friends do and endure on our behalf are in a sense our own deeds and sufferings, for friendship is a mutual power uniting two persons and making them somehow one. For this reason a man may be justly discharged because his friend has made restitution."(40) [75]

Post-Reformation Non-Catholic theologians generally called this Substitutionary Expiation.

Vicarious Expiation can also be a concept too difficult to understand. But we must try to understand it if we are to understand the reasoning for the Incarnation, Death, Burial and Resurrection of Jesus the Christ. And it explains the concept of Divine Mercy.

Vicarious expiation is found in the Story of the Binding of Isaac where God supplies Abraham with a ram to save Isaac from being sacrificed. [76] We find it in the Hebrew Feast of *Kippurim* (*Yom Kippur*), in which a goat was killed and its blood sprinkled on people and the Mercy Seat as a sign of purification and reconciliation with God. We find this feast in Leviticus 16: 16 and Hebrews 9: 19-28. Isaiah 53: 10-11 predicted that the future Messiah (Jesus, the Christ) would be the expiatory Victim, the Suffering Servant, for the sins of men.

Now we can begin to understand the wonderful quote from St. Augustine used during the Holy Saturday Easter Vigil, and sung in the Easter Proclamation, the *Exsultet*:

> "Father, how wonderful your care for us! How boundless your merciful Love! To ransom a slave you gave away your Son. Which gained for us so great a Redeemer! O happy fault, O necessary sin of Adam, [77]

---

75 Conference transcription from a talk that Father John Hardon gave to the Institute on Religious Life, Chapter VIII, Christology of Thomas Aquinas found at http://www.therealpresence.org/archives/Christology

76 Genesis 22: 1-19

77 *Exultet*, Easter Vigil

O happy fault? O necessary sin of Adam? How can any sin be called necessary? How can any fault be called happy? It can because God's mercy stays or holds back His justice while God puts into place His plan of redemption through *vicarious expiation* – something totally unexpected for man.

Because of the sin of our first parents, we do not walk with God in the Garden of Eden in the cool of the evening. But unexpectedly, because the God Man shed His blood for us, we participate in the Divine Life in a way the Adam and Eve did not.

St. Paul says:

"But however much sin increased, grace was always greater." [78]

And because of the results of Jesus the Christ's death according to God the Father's Plan, we are not just friends walking with God in the Garden, but more than friends, as Paul says:

"But when the completion of the time came, God sent his Son, born of a woman, born a subject of the Law, to redeem the subjects of the Law, so that we could receive adoption as sons. As you are sons, God has sent into our hearts the Sprit of his Son crying, 'Abba, Father', and so you are no longer a slave, but a son; and if a son, then an heir, by God's own act." [79]

We are now more than friends. We are sons and heirs!

Here, then is the mercy of God at work. Here then is the reason for the Incarnation. God who is infinite perfection could not and would not abide sin, which is the epitome of IM-perfection. God abhors sin. If God were guided by Justice alone, He might have annihilated man immediately after the first sin, or, at least, condemned man forever as he did the rebellious angels as St. Peter says:

"When angels sinned, God did not spare them: he sent them down into the underworld and consigned them to the dark abyss to be held there until the Judgment." [80]

Shouldn't man, who has made himself infinitely abhorrent to God because of sin, receive more than just being banished from the Garden of Eden or

---

78   Romans 5: 21a
79   Galatians 4: 4-7
80   2 Peter 2: 4

God's presence? Shouldn't man find that God would seek to annihilate him by bringing instant death and destruction? God didn't take life away from the fallen angels since they are spiritual and not corporeal (material) beings and were created to be immortal.

But man did not die immediately physically. Although man experiences the loss of his preternatural gifts, [81] we find that something LESS than instant death and the destruction of man takes place. Man is banished, given temporal sufferings and temporal death. Here we see that mercy is infinitely greater than justice is, since the punishment exacted is smaller than the infinite guilt.

And by prophetic utterance, God, because of His infinite love for His fallen creatures, mercifully foretells that eventually there will be the means for restoration and reunion through the action of the vicarious expiation of His only Begotten Son, the Second Person of the Blessed Trinity, the God Man, Jesus, the Christ. John tells us this in his Gospel:

> "For this is how God loved the world: he gave his only Son, so that everyone who believes in him say not perish but may have eternal life. [17] For God sent his Son into the world not to judge the world, but so that through him the world might be saved." [82]

"God is Love," as St. John says. [83] But this love directed toward fallen human beings in their misery, is not Love, but Mercy says St. Thomas Aquinas in his *Summa Theologiae*:

> "By way of explanation we note that a person is called merciful because he has a heart with misery, and is affected with sadness for another's plight as though it were his own. He identifies himself with the other, and springs to the rescue; this is the effect of mercy. To feel sad about another's misery is *no* attribute of God, but to drive it out is supremely his, and by misery we mean here any sort of defect. Defects are not

---

81   "That which surpasses nature, its laws and its active and passive potency or capacity... In the state of original innocence sanctifying grace and the infused virtues (*supernatural gifts*) must be distinguished from an aggregate of *preternatural gifts*, which constitute the *integrity* of human nature (bodily immortality, infused knowledge, and immunity from concupiscence)." Parente, Pietro, et al. *Dictionary of Dogmatic Theology* (Milwaukee: Bruce, 1952) pp. 227-8.

82   John 3: 16-17

83   I John 4: 8

done away with save by an achievement of goodness. And, as we have said, God is the first source of goodness." [84]

John Paul II says it this way in his encyclical, *Dives in Misericordia*, or *Rich in Mercy*, which was published earlier in his pontificate, in 1980:

"Believing in the crucified Son means 'seeing the Father,' means believing that love is present in the world and that this love is more powerful than any kind of evil in which individuals, humanity, or the world are involved. Believing in this love means believing in mercy. For mercy is an indispensable dimension of love; it is as it were love's second name, and, at the same time, it is the specific manner in which love is revealed and effected..." [85]

Justice defers to merciful love as the Epistle of St. James says:

"Whoever acts without mercy will be judged without mercy, but mercy can afford to laugh at judgment." [86]

In God's Divine Plan we find that when God begins to seek out and to relate to mankind again, He reveals Himself by the attribute which is most prominently manifested in the story of His relationship with Adam and Eve in the Garden of Eden. In this seeking out and beginning a new relationship with Man, God does not identify Himself as the *Loving God*. God identifies Himself as the *Merciful God*!

We find this in the *Exodus* story. Working through Moses to free the children of Israel from the slavery of Pharaoh, God develops a very personal relationship with Moses. It shows us what God wanted with Adam and Eve in the Garden of Eden. God's relationship with Moses is so intense that later on God identifies Moses as His Friend:

"Yahweh would talk to Moses face to face, as a man talks to his friend, and afterwards he would come back to the camp..." [87]

When a friend asks you intimate questions about yourself or when a friend asks to share your secret things, you willingly open up yourself and

84 Aquinas, St. Thomas, *op.cit.*, 1A, q. 21, 3 (2). p. 145
85 John Paul II, *Dives in Misericordia*, Part V, Article 7, (Boston, MA, Daughters of St. Paul) 1980, p. 26
86 James 2: 13
87 Exodus 33: 11

those secret things to your friend. As Moses works for and with Yahweh in freeing His people for slavery, Moses also begins to seek to know God more intimately. Therefore Moses asks:

"'Please show me your glory.'" [88]

Yahweh answers Moses this way:

"'I shall make all my goodness pass before you, and before you I shall pronounce the name Yahweh; and I am gracious to those to whom I am gracious and I take pity on those on whom I take pity. [20] But my face', he said, 'you cannot see, for no human being can see me and survive.' [21] Then Yahweh said, 'Here is a place near me. You will stand on the rock, [22] and when my glory passes by, I shall put you in a cleft of the rock and shield you with my hand until I have gone past. [23] Then I shall take my hand away and you will see my back; but my face will not be seen.'" [89]

In chapter 34, when Yahweh finally passes before Moses pronouncing His Name, notice what description God gives of Himself. It is all about Mercy!

"Then Yahweh passed before him and called out, 'Yahweh, Yahweh, God of tenderness and compassion, slow to anger, rich in faithful love and constancy, [7] maintaining his faithful love to thousands, forgiving fault, crime and sin, yet letting nothing go unchecked, and punishing the parent's fault in the children and in the grandchildren to the third and fourth generation!'" [90]

Moses understands God's words as announcing His greatest attribute or character. This greatest attribute God states in a series of words. His attribute is so rich in meaning that one word does not do justice to His attribute. God states He is a God of *tenderness, compassion, slow to anger, faithful love and constancy.*

Tenderness comes from (7349 רחום *rechum* from 7355) [91] the Hebrew word meaning full of compassion and mercy. *Compassion* comes from (2587 חכניך *channun* from 2603) the Hebrew word which means to stoop in kindness to

---

88   Exodus 33: 18
89   Exodus 33: 18-23
90   Exodus 34: : 6-8
91   The numbers after a Hebrew or Greek word indicates the reference number in *Strong's Exhaustive Concordance of the Bible.*

an inferior. *Slow to anger* come from (750 & 639 אף ארך *arek* & *aph* from 748) the Hebrew words meaning to be long drawn out (from 599) or to delay being displeased. *Faithful love* comes from (2617 חסד *chesed* the Hebrew word for pity or mercy. *Constancy* comes from (571 אמת *emeth* from 539 *aman*) the word Hebrew meaning to be faithful or trustworthy.

If we put the descriptions together with the repetition of His name, Yahweh, I AM HE WHO IS, we get a sentence that goes like this:

"I AM HE WHO IS, I AM HE WHO IS FULL OF COMPASSION, STOOPING IN KINDNESS TO AN INFERIOR, DRAWING OUT AND DELAYING MY DISPLEASURE AND ANGER BECAUSE OF MY PITY AND MERCY SINCE I AM FAITHFUL AND TRUSTWORTHY."

One word cannot contain all the levels of meaning and nuances of the attribute of God as Merciful. In the Hebrew, God used six different words to describe His Name as MERCY.

This becomes more difficult and confusing when we try translating these six Hebrew words into English. There is no single English word adequate to impart the full meaning of each Hebrew word. So combinations are used: Loving kindness, heartfelt love, merciful love, faithful love, and steadfast love.

How many times and in how many words does God repeat Himself to make us understand that His Mercy exceeds His justice?

God continues to explain to Moses that His faithful love is not to one person, but to thousands. God explains that He is forgiving of fault, crime and sin, yet His Justice demands that nothing goes unchecked or unpunished.

Moses' response and reply show he understands what God has said about Himself and His Nature. Moses understands that God has said that He is Mercy itself.

Therefore Moses' reaction is most important for us:

"[8] Moses immediately bowed to the ground in worship, [9] then he said, 'If indeed I do enjoy your favour, please, my Lord, come with us, although they are an obstinate people; and forgive our faults and sins, and adopt us as your heritage.' [92]

Moses invites God to be part of this stiff necked, stubborn people because God is forgiving and merciful and the people are obstinate.

Pope John Paul II in his encyclical *Rich in Mercy* says:

92   Exodus 34: 9

"Added to this is the fact that sin too constitutes man's misery. The people of the Old Covenant experienced this misery from the time of the exodus, when they set up the golden calf. The Lord Himself triumphed over this act of breaking the covenant when He solemnly declared to Moses that He was a 'God merciful and gracious, slow to anger, and abounding in steadfast love and faithfulness.' It is in this central revelation that the chosen people, and each of its members, will find, every time that they have sinned, the strength and the motive for turning to the Lord to remind Him of what He has exactly revealed about Himself and to beseech His forgiveness." [93]

From this point on, God's identifies Himself in Scripture through His perfection or attribute of Mercy when He relates to this people whom He has saved by bringing them out of slavery.

We all easily recognize God as Creator, Redeemer and Sanctifier: the Father, Son and Holy Spirit. But *GOD* identifies with us by His attribute of Mercy: his pitying our misery and satisfying our needs. Throughout scripture, the word mercy is so identified with God that in understanding Mercy we grow in understanding something about God's nature.

The whole concept of Mercy and what it includes is most beautifully explained by God in His discourse with Ezekiel concerning the role of the prophet as watchman:

"Son of man, say to the House of Israel, 'You are continually saying: Our crimes and sins weigh heavily on us; we are wasting away because of them. How are we to go on living?' Say to them, 'As I live—declares the Lord Yahweh—I do not take pleasure in the death of the wicked but in the conversion of the wicked who changes his ways and saves his life. Repent, turn back from your evil ways. Why die, House of Israel?" [94]

Therefore, because of God's explanation in Old Testament about His merciful Nature scripture verses in the New Testament take on meanings at a deeper level.

In the Gospel of Luke after Jesus gives the Beatitudes he continues to talk about loving our enemies and ends by saying:

"Be merciful just as your Father is merciful. Do not judge, and you

---

93   John Paul II, *op.cit.*, Article 4, page 15
94   Ezekiel 33: 10-11

will not be judged; do not condemn, and you will not be condemned; forgive, and you will be forgiven." [95]

Jesus is telling us to be like His Father Who allows His mercy to do its work before His judgment and condemnation take effect.

St. Paul in Romans then tells us how God Mercy works for us:

"So it is proof of God's own love for us, that Christ died for us while we were still sinners." [96]

God's mercy is not just something He decided to exercise at one particular time or event. Whereas, human mercy is dependent upon *our* love of neighbor. His mercy is unlimited and infinite. Therefore, it cannot be dependent upon anyone or anything, since God is immutable, that is, unchangeable. He is always perfectly merciful.

God is Life itself (*Yahweh*: I AM HE WHO IS). Then Life is His greatest gift. Since death is the absence of Life, God's desire is that Man be restored to life. Jesus said to Philip:

"Have I been with you all this time, Philip, and you still do not know me? Anyone who has seen me has seen the Father." [97]

Jesus said in the Gospel of John:

"The thief comes only to steal and kill and destroy. I have come so that they may have life and have it to the full. I am the good shepherd: the good shepherd lays down his life for his sheep." [98]

In his encyclical, *Rich in Mercy*, Pope John Paul II explains that God's most stupendous attribute is mercy! He also says *"Love's second name is Mercy."* [99]

St. Thomas Aquinas in his *Summa Theologiae* goes so far as to say that God's Mercy is a higher perfection than His Love. St. Thomas says God's Mercy is the greater perfection since Mercy is the communicating or extending one's own perfection to another. God does this by bringing man from his own

---

95   Luke 6: 36-37
96   Romans 5: 8
97   John 14: 9
98   John 10: 10-11
99   John Paul II, op.cit., Part V, Article 7, p. 26.

misery and wretchedness by removing man's imperfection and *elevating man to Himself.* [100]

Jesus was sent by the Father to redeem mankind. As the God Man, perfectly God and perfectly Man, Infinite and Finite, he could make appropriate expiation for our sins. Since He did it perfectly, it does not have to be repeated, but is effective and sufficient forever. Therefore, St. Paul in his Epistle to the Hebrews 10: 11-14 says this about the completeness of Christ's Sacrifice:

"Every priest stands at his duties every day, offering over and over again the same sacrifices which are quite incapable of taking away sins. [12] He, on the other hand, has offered one single sacrifice for sins, and then taken his seat for ever, at the right hand of God, [13] where he is now waiting till his enemies are made his footstool. [14] By virtue of that one single offering, he has achieved the eternal perfection of all who are sanctified." [101]

The Book of Ruth also tells us about the *kinsman redeemer*! The kinsman redeemer is an idea peculiar to the Hebrew people. When great famine came, or financial disaster hit a family, it might become necessary for the family to sell off all the property that it possessed. Sometimes they even sold themselves into servitude. If this happened, then according the Leviticus 25: 25, it became the right and the duty for the male next of kin to perform a specific act to insure the preservation of the family land or the name of the deceased male relative. The root for the word *"next of kin"* or *"next kinsman"* (go'el) (גאל) (1350) (is from the Hebrew word which means to *"redeem,"* or *"to buy back."*

"You will allow a right of redemption over any ancestral property. [25] If your brother becomes impoverished and sells off part of his ancestral property, his nearest male relative will come and exercise his family rights over what his brother has sold. [26] The man who has no one to exercise this right may, once he has found the means to effect the redemption, [27] calculate the number of years that the alienation would have lasted, repay to the purchaser the sum due for the time still to run, and so recover his ancestral property. [28] If he cannot find the sum in compensation, the property sold will remain in the possession

---

100 Aquinas, St. Thomas, *Summa Theologiae*, I, q 21, aa. 3 and 4; II-II, q 20, a. 4. p. 145
101 Hebrews 10: 11-14

of the purchaser until the jubilee year. In the jubilee year, the latter will vacate it and return to his own ancestral property." [102]

In this *go'el* is the *"avenger of the blood,"* the victim's nearest male relative. This is a private vengeance system which exists today among some desert tribes. If a man is murdered, then the oldest male relative must avenge his blood.

"The avenger of blood will put the murderer to death. Whenever he finds him, he will put him to death." [103]

The combination of both ideas (the redeemer kinsman and the avenger of the blood) is seen very well in Psalm 19: 14 (*"Yahweh, my rock, my redeemer"*); Isaiah 41: 14 (*"I shall help you, declares Yahweh; your redeemer is the Holy One of Israel"*); and Jeremiah 50: 34 (*"But your redeemer is strong: Yahweh Sabaoth is his name."*), where God is called the *go'el* or redeemer of Israel. This is a true sense of the Divine Protection where Yahweh is avenger, Savior, rescuer and redeemer of his people from death.

The meaning becomes very powerful when you understand that it is the basis of Isaiah's *"Second Song of the Servant,"* [104] which is applied to the Messiah. If the Messiah is the *"go'el"*, then he is truly the protector and vindicator of the helpless or hapless members of his family.

"And now Yahweh has spoken, who formed me in the womb to be his servant, to bring Jacob back to him and to re-unite Israel to him; —I shall be honoured in Yahweh's eyes, and my God has been my strength. — [6] He said, 'It is not enough for you to be my servant, to restore the tribes of Jacob and bring back the survivors of Israel; I shall make you a light to the nations so that my salvation may reach the remotest parts of earth.'[7] Thus says Yahweh, the redeemer, the Holy One of Israel, to the one who is despised, detested by the nation, to the slave of despots: Kings will stand up when they see, princes will see and bow low, because of Yahweh who is faithful, the Holy One of Israel who has chosen you." [105]

There is a merging here of the levirate law and the law of the *go'el* found in Leviticus:

---

102 Leviticus 25: 24-28
103 Numbers 35: 19
104 Isaiah 49: 1-7
105 Isaiah 49: 5-7

"If your brother becomes impoverished and sells off part of his ancestral property, his nearest male relative will come and exercise his family rights over what his brother has sold. [26] The man who has no one to exercise this right may, once he has found the means to effect the redemption, [27] calculate the number of years that the alienation would have lasted, repay to the purchaser the sum due for the time still to run, and so recover his ancestral property. [28] If he cannot find the sum in compensation, the property sold will remain in the possession of the purchaser until the jubilee year. In the jubilee year, the latter will vacate it and return to his own ancestral property." [106]

Eventually this practice, the redemption of the land, fell into disrepute among the Jews. Obviously, the wealthy who may have acquired land and property in shady dealings didn't want a redemption/jubilee restoration hanging in the balance. Can you imagine the consternation and confusion at the first jubilee year when people were expecting their ancestral properties to be returned to them? And wouldn't that be something today, if we truly believed that God owned everything and was just lending it to us? Not only the land, but everything: the gold and the silver!

The other thing that is significant about the process of the redemption by the kinsman of the widow in order to continue the deceased male kinsman's name, is that the *go'el* is required to marry the widow and raise up children to his brother and keep his kinsman's name alive. That doesn't speak to a monogamous marriage custom, but then the Lord was interested in the continuance of the lineage and inheritance. God doesn't want a line cut off, therefore he protects the widow who no longer has the protection of a supporting male.

The rabbis have always related The Feast of Pentecost to the Law-Giving on Mount Sinai. The Law or Covenant is the Marriage Contract (*Ketubah*) (כתובה) between God and Israel.

Exodus 19:1 states that after 3 months of leaving Egypt the people came to Mount Sinai. Since they left Egypt in the middle of the First Month, then their arrival at Mount Sinai and the giving of the Law or Marriage Contract coincided with the Feast of Pentecost. Even to this day, Jews draw up a marriage contract or a *Ketubah* (כתובה). The Scroll of "Jubilees" from Qumran, explicitly states this relationship between Pentecost and the Giving of the Law, and the Marriage of Israel to Yahweh. Let us look at this in a spiritual or mystical sense. Christ, the anointed one, the chosen one, in the sense of Isaiah 41:

---

106 Leviticus 25: 25-28

"Do not be afraid, Jacob, you worm! You little handful of Israel! I shall help you, declares Yahweh; your redeemer is the Holy One of Israel." [107]

He is a kinsman (*Go'el*) to us now. He has taken on human flesh and is our brother. His humanity comes through the line directly from Adam. So even from a biological point of view we are all related to Christ, as we are related to every other human being, albeit very distantly. Since He is the First Born Son of God, and the heir to everything, He is more than capable of acting as "*go'el*" for we poor hapless and helpless relatives who have been sold into slavery by our father, Adam. Jesus, whose name means savior, redeems us with his blood, in a unique twist of the *"avenger of the blood."* [108]

The mystical aspect takes on unbelievable nuances when we understand that all of us are now parts of his body, the Mystical Body of Christ, the Church, the Bride, and that he is going to purify that body. And, the Mystical Body of Christ, the Church, when it is *"without spot and wrinkle,"* [109] it will be His Bride and He as the New Adam, will raise us up children, albeit adopted sons, to God.

This then is Divine Mercy. Divine Mercy is the Father's Plan of Salvation: The Redemption, Resurrection, and Restoration of fallen Mankind by the God-Man, Jesus, the Christ:

- God who created Man and gave him life also gave man another great Gift: a free will. With a free will, man has the ability to say NO to God.
- Adam and Eve, our parents, did just that. They said NO to God by disobeying Him.
- God's justice demanded punishment which was death.
- God's love looked on man's misery and in pity God's Mercy held back His hand of Justice and death was delayed.
- God's love, working with His Mercy, put into action His Plan of the Redeemer, the Vicarious Expiation, by promising a Messiah (or anointed one) who would do God's will completely as the Suffering Servant in Isaiah 53.
- In the fullness of time Jesus, the Christ, was born of the Virgin Mary and was like us in all things, except sin.

---

107   Isaiah 41: 14
108   Numbers 35: 19
109   Ephesians 5: 27

- Perfectly God and Perfectly Man, both Infinite and Finite, as our Brother, He became our Redeemer Kinsman (go'el) (לגאל), [110] took our sins upon Himself, died for us as the Vicarious Expiation.
- God's Plan of Salvation through His Attribute of Mercy now sees that His justice is satisfied.
- But we now find that *the unexpected.*
- For mankind is not just restored to the Friendship of God. We are made sons and heirs with His only Son Jesus, the Christ.

To celebrate this great mystery of the Mercy of God and His Plan of Salvation for Mankind, the Church now celebrates the Sunday after Easter as Mercy Sunday.

I will close my introduction to the meaning of mercy by quoting the Church's opening prayer from the Mass of the 2nd Sunday of Easter, Mercy Sunday:

"Heavenly Father and God of Mercy, We no longer look for Jesus among the dead, for He is alive and has become the Lord of Life.

From the waters of death you raised us with him and renew your gift of life within us.

Increase in our minds and hearts the risen life we share with Christ and help us to grow as your people toward the fullness of eternal life with you.

We ask this through Christ our Lord. Amen

---

110 *Catechism of the Catholic Church*, 618: "Our participation in Christ's sacrifice. The cross is the unique sacrifice of Christ, the "one mediator between God and men."(1 Timothy 2: 5) *But because in his incarnate divine person he has in some way united himself to every man*, "the possibility of being made partners, in a way known to God, in the paschal mystery" is offered to all men. (GS 22 5; cf. 2) He calls his disciples to "take up [their] cross and follow [him],"(Matthew 16: 24) for *"Christ also suffered for [us]*, leaving [us] an example so that [we] should follow in his steps."(1 Peter 2: 21) In fact Jesus desires to associate with his redeeming sacrifice those who were to be its first beneficiaries. (Cf. Mark 10: 29; John 21: 18-10; Colossians 1: 24) This is achieved supremely in the case of his mother, who was associated more intimately than any other person in the mystery of his redemptive suffering. (Cf. Luke 2: 35)

Chapter 4
The Chaplet of Divine Mercy

Introduction to Chapter 4
The Chaplet of Divine Mercy

When Dr. Robert Stackpole asked me to do a talk on the Chaplet of Divine Mercy at the John Paul II Institute of Divine Mercy's *"An Ocean of Mercy"* seminar in Houston, Texas in September 3-6, 1999, I responded that I didn't want to do it. I arrogantly declined because everyone knew about the Chaplet. Dr. Stackpole prevailed upon me to do the talk. I am forever indebted to him for "twisting my arm".

As I did my research I began to realize that I was praying the Chaplet of Divine Mercy and I didn't know much about it. It wasn't until I seriously began to re-read and study the *Diary of St. Faustina* for the seminar talk that I began to understand the power of the Chaplet.

After I presented my talk, Fr. Seraphim Michalenko, stated: "That is the most definitive talk on the Chaplet that I have heard." I had to go back to my recordings of the sessions to convince myself that that is what he actually said.

Since 1999 I have done extensive research into the Chaplet as additional information became available, especially from recently translated Polish sources.

One of the greatest finds I discovered was *when* and *why* the Chaplet was *dictated* by Jesus. I have found additional information from the personal writings of Blessed Father Michael Sopocko, and the publication of the personal letters of St. Faustina and also Maria Tarnawska' great biography: *Sister Faustina Kowalska – her life and mission.*

Anyone in pro-life ministry or who supports the same must know the information in this chapter.

The Chaplet of Divine Mercy

Unlike the Rosary, the Chaplet has no history of growth into its present form and structure. Its present form and structure is the same as when it was given by Jesus to Sr. Faustina on September 13, 1935. [111] That is very important for two reasons.

First, there is no *human* manipulation of its concept, form or structure. It came to us full-blown and mature. To this day it is exactly as Jesus wanted and directed from the beginning. By that I mean, that everything that surrounds it and the graces that flow from it are *not man inspired by his prayer life*, but *God directed and fulfilled*.

Second, although the Chaplet is similar in structure to the Rosary, it is *not dependent* upon it. However, it does derive support from its association with the Rosary.

Then a logical question is "If it is to be said on the Rosary beads, why is it not called the Rosary of Divine Mercy?"

That question is at the heart of the differences and similarities between the whole tradition of the Rosary of the Blessed Virgin Mary and the origin of the Chaplet of Divine Mercy. We need to understand the history and origin of the Rosary in order to understand what the Chaplet *is* and *is not*.

The most popular view of the origin of the rosary is that at the beginning of the 13th century St. Dominic received the rosary in a vision from the Blessed Virgin Mary. However, there are no records to support the claim St. Dominic received the rosary directly from Mary: nothing in his own writings, nothing in the archives of the order, nothing in the documents involved in his canonization, nor in any of the early biographies about him.

However, there is a secular history that states it is the result of the Crusaders who saw the Muslims using strung beads or knotted cords as devices for

---

111   Diary Entry 476

counting prayers. Then the Crusaders adapted the beads for Christian prayers and brought them back to Europe in the 12th Century.

Actually, the history of the rosary is more complex than that. The practice of using beads or knotted strings or pebbles to count prayers seems to be a universal practice. We can find it in many religions, in many countries, in many different cultures, and in different times in man's history.

Among the early mentions of prayer beads in England is the will of Lady Godiva. She actually did exist (although her naked ride through Coventry is mythical) and died about 1040. John Miller writes in his book, Beads & Prayers:

> "It is in the eleventh century that we have the first firm reference to the use of prayter beads in England. It is stated by William of Malmesbury that the Lady Godiva of Coventry, wife of Count Leofric, bequeathed to the monastery which they had founded 'a circlet of gems which she had threaded on a string, in order that by fingering them one by one as she successively recited her prayers she might not fall short of the exact number'" [112]

Note: this precedes the Crusades by 50 years and St. Dominic by almost 200 years. [113]

What prayers were recited on these first "rosaries?"

In the Church's official prayer, the Divine Office, or the Liturgy of the Hours, at the time of beginning of the Rosary, the 150 psalms were recited over the course of one week. (The four-week Psalter came after Vatican II.) The ordinary folk could not read nor did they have the time to memorize all 150 psalms. So they substituted the most commonly known prayer, the *Our Father*, for each of the psalms. This custom became known in Europe as the *"Poor Man's Office."*

Rosaries were first known as *"Pater Nosters."* To this day there is a street in London where they made these rosaries and the name of that street is *"Pater Noster Row."*

Why were "Pater Nosters" or "Our Fathers" said on the beads and not "Ave Maria's" or "Hail Mary's" as today?

The "Hail Mary" in its present form is of more recent origin. Historically we find the linking of the greeting of the Archangel Gabriel *"Hail, Full of Grace, the Lord is with you,"* with the greeting of St. Elizabeth: *"Blessed are you among women and blessed is the fruit of your womb"* in the Eastern Church in

112 John D. Miller, *Beads & Prayers*, (London: Burns & Oates 2002), p. 89
113 Kevin Orlin Johnson, *Why Do Catholics Do That?* (New York: Ballantine 1994), p. 97.

the Greek Liturgy of St. James in the 5th Century. And a short time later we find it in the Latin Liturgy used in Rome.

It is not until the 11th Century, in a work attributed to St. Peter Damian, that we find the story of a person who is described as praying each day: *"Hail, full of grace, the Lord is with thee; blessed are thou among women, and blessed is the fruit of thy womb."* Sometime *later* the names of "Mary" and "Jesus" were added.

The second part of the Ave Maria grew gradually in different forms. One 14th Century addition reads: *"Oh Blessed Virgin, pray to God for us always, that He may pardon us and give us grace, so to live here below that He may reward us with paradise at our death."*

The words of conclusion that we are more familiar with: *"Holy Mary, mother of God, pray for us sinners,"* dates from 1493, one year after the discovery of America.

Sometime after this, the practice grew to meditate on the mysteries of our faith or events in the lives of Jesus and Mary. We find in the middle of the 1400's that a Carthusian monk compiled a list of 50 mysteries on which to meditate, in conjunction with the recitation of 50 Hail Mary's.

The whole cult of the Rosary received great impetus with the formation of the Confraternity of the Rosary, founded by a Dominican in 1470.

A book published in 1489 describes the rosary as we know it today. It consisted of 15 decades of an Our Father and 10 Hail Mary's each. [114] A mystery was given to each decade. The 15 mysteries are the same as ours today except the Coronation of Mary as queen of heaven was joined with her Assumption in the fourth glorious mystery. This version's fifth glorious mystery was the Last Judgment.

A crucial event in the History of Europe solidified the Cult of the Rosary. On the First Sunday of October in 1571, the Christian forces from Europe defeated the Turkish fleet in the Naval Battle of Lepanto. As the battle was raging the Confraternities of the Rosary in Rome were holding processions and reciting the rosary as a prayer for victory at the urging of Pope St. Pius V, a Dominican. In gratitude for the victory, Pope St. Pius V established the Feast of The Holy Rosary in 1573. Pope Clement XI made it universal in 1716.

We do owe a debt to a Dominican for the Confraternity of the Rosary. We do owe a debt to a Dominican for the Feast of the Most Holy Rosary: Pope St. Pius V.

The changes in the Rosary did not stop there. We know from Sr. Lucia that during the August 19, 1917 apparition the Blessed Mother honors this prayer form that has grown from the spirituality of the laity, and asked that

---

114 *Ibid.*, p.100.

the following prayer be added at the end of each decade of the Rosary after the recitation of the *Glory Be*:

> "O my Jesus, forgive us our sins. Save us from the fire of hell, and lead all souls to Heaven, especially those most in need of Thy mercy."

The latest addition to the Cult of the Rosary is the Luminous Mysteries added in 2003 by Pope John Paul II now making it 20 mysteries instead of 15.

Now my questions is: Why is the Rosary called a rosary and why is the Chaplet called the chaplet?

In the early 1300s when the Hail Mary's were added to the Our Father's and the cult of Mary increased. It was called a *"Rosarium"* or Rose garden. It applied equally to any Marian *devotional* group and not to the *beads* themselves.

The New Webster's Dictionary (Deluxe Encyclopedia Edition) gives this information about a rosary:

> "from the Latin *rosarium*, a rose garden. Catholic Church: a sequence or series of prayers and devotions divided into 15 decades or groups of ten each; a string of beads, joined to a crucifix, used to count and separate the sequence of such prayers; such as string of beads with five decades; prayer beads. Among other religious bodies, a string of beads, similarly used in prayer. A rose garden; a bed of roses."

There are multiple stories of why it is called a Rose Garden. My favorite (and because it is my favorite, I will use it): Mary is the *Mystical Rose* who gave birth to Jesus, the *Rose of Sharon*. By saying our *"rosary"* with Mary, we are gathered under her mantel as in a secret garden. [115] And as we pray we become more like her son and we too exude a sweet odor like Jesus, the *Rose of Sharon*, as Paul says *"To God we are the fragrance of Christ..."* [116]

What then is a chaplet? *The New Webster's Dictionary* (Deluxe Encyclopedia Edition) gives this definition:

> "from the French, *chapelet*, a diminutive from *"chapel"* meaning a head dress. A wreath or garland for the head; a string of beads; a string of beads for counting prayers, one third of the length of a rosary; the prayers so counted; anything resembling a string of beads..."

---

115 See Song of Songs 4: 12
116 2 Corinthians 2: 15

By identifying the formula of prayers as a chaplet said on rosary beads, Jesus gives the structure of the Chaplet of Divine Mercy as 1/3 the length of the full rosary. The chaplet proper is comprised of 5 decades, each decade having an introductory prayer and a following prayer repeated 10 times, once on each bead of the decade.

Let us now begin to compare the order of prayers in the Chaplet of Divine Mercy and those of the Rosary.

In the first major entry concerning The Chaplet of Divine Mercy St. Faustina tells us Jesus' description of what prayers are used in this Chaplet:

> "The next morning, when I entered chapel, I heard these words interiorly: **Every time you enter the chapel, immediately** *recite the prayer which I taught you yesterday.* When I had said the prayer, in my soul I heard these words: **This prayer will serve to appease My wrath. You will recite it for nine days, on the beads of the rosary, in the following manner: First of all, you will say one OUR FATHER and HAIL MARY and the I BELIEVE IN GOD. Then on the OUR FATHER beads you will say the following words: "Eternal Father, I offer You the Body and Blood, Soul and Divinity of Your dearly beloved Son, Our Lord Jesus Christ, in atonement for our sins and those of the whole world." On the HAIL MARY beads you will say the following words: "For the sake of His sorrowful Passion have mercy on us and on the whole world." In conclusion, three times you will recite these words: "Holy God, Holy Mighty One, Holy Immortal One, have mercy on us and on the whole world."** [117]

This prayer that Jesus says He taught Sr. Faustina "yesterday" is:

> "The words with which I entreated God are these:
> **Eternal Father, I offer You the Body and Blood, Soul and Divinity of Your dearly beloved Son, Our Lord Jesus Christ for our sins and those of the whole world; for the sake of His sorrowful passion, have mercy on us."** [118]

This prayer is the chief prayer of the chaplet, and it helps us to understand the differences and similarities between the Chaplet of Divine Mercy and the Rosary.

The Rosary, as we know it today, begins with the *Apostles Creed*, followed

---

117   Diary Entry 476
118   *Ibid.*, Entry 475

by the *Our Father,* Three *Hail Mary's,* and one *Glory Be,* as the introduction to the decades of the Mysteries [119].

The Chaplet of Divine Mercy has a reverse order in its introduction.

By direction of Jesus, it begins with the *Our Father,* followed by *ONE Hail Mary,* then the *Apostles Creed* without a *Glory Be.*

This change in formula is most important and emphasizes the difference in the power and effectiveness of the Chaplet of Divine Mercy in comparison to the Rosary.

The Rosary is designed to be a Faith builder. Sr. Lucia in her own handwriting in a letter to Mother Martins on September 16, 1970, said this about the Rosary as a faith builder:

> "Unfortunately, we cannot hopefully expect a great number of souls to assist at daily Mass, but we can hope to bring a greater number of them to recite the daily Rosary. This practice will preserve and increase their faith, due to the prayer life it fosters and to the mysteries of our redemption which are remembered in each decade. The Rosary is the prayer of the poor and the rich, of the wise and the ignorant. To uproot this devotion from souls is to deprive them of their daily spiritual bread. The Rosary helps to preserve that flickering flame of faith that has not yet been completely extinguished from many consciences..." [120]

By *meditating* on the Mysteries [121] of the Life of Jesus Christ in association with the Life of Mary our *faith is strengthened.*

---

119 "Mysteries of the rosary are those events in the lives of Jesus and His Mother, Mary, upon which one is to meditate while reciting the prayers of the Rosary, either privately or publicly. (There are now twenty mysteries, one for each of the twenty decades of the Rosary.) "Each subject should be spoken or thought of before beginning decade and, according to the practice of meditation, kept in mind during the recitation of the prayers." Cf. *The Catholic Encyclopedia,* Robert Broderick, editor (Nashville, TN: Thomas Nelson Publishers, 1987), p.406.

120 *The Rosary and the Crisis of Faith,* Msgr. Joseph A. Cirrincione and Thomas A. Nelson. TAN, 1986), pp. 15-6.

121 The *Joyful* Mysteries: the Annunciation, Visitation, Nativity, Presentation and Finding of Jesus in the Temple. The *Sorrowful* Mysteries: the Agony in the Garden, the Scourging, the Crowning with Thorns, the Carrying of the Cross, and the Crucifixion. The *Luminous* Mysteries: The Baptism of Jesus, the Wedding Feast at Cana, the Proclamation of the Good News, the Transfiguration, the Institution of the Eucharist. The *Glorious* Mysteries: The Resurrection, the Ascension, the Descent of the Holy Spirit, the Assumption

Meditation is best described in the Catechism:

> "Meditation engages thought, imagination, emotion, and desire. This mobilization of faculties is necessary in order to deepen our convictions of faith, prompt the conversion of our heart, and strengthen our will to follow Christ. Christian prayer tries above all to *meditate* on the mysteries of Christ, as in *lectio divina* or the *ROSARY*. This form of prayerful reflection is of great value, but Christian prayer should go further: to the knowledge of the love of the Lord Jesus, to union with him." [122]

Therefore, the Rosary as a meditative prayer begins with an acknowledgement of our beliefs given in the Apostles Creed. Those faith beliefs begin with *"I believe."* Faith is an individual's assent of the will.

In order to put us in the right *Christian* frame of mind, we must go beyond the individual into the community. The Rosary next goes to the Prayer Jesus taught us that identifies us as Christians: *The Our Father*. *The Our Father* helps to form community. It is all first person plural pronouns: *"Our"* and *"us,"* and not *"I"* and *"we"* or *"mine"* and *"my"*.

Since the family is the earthly representation of the Heavenly Community of the Triune God, as part of the family on earth the mother of the family must also get involved. Mary, our mother, gets involved with the *Hail Mary*.

The *Hail Mary* is repeated three times in order to build up our theological virtues of Faith, Hope and Love. Once built up with Faith, Hope and Love, we spontaneously enter into the praise of the Triune God with the *Glory Be*. Thus, we are prepared to begin our mediation on the mysteries of the Life of Jesus Christ in Association with the Life of Mary as we enter the decades of the mysteries.

This understanding of the Introduction to the Rosary is also the key to understanding the Chaplet of Divine Mercy.

The Chaplet is *not* a meditation, but a *prayer of petition*. It is a very special form of petition called *INTERCESSION*. The Catechism of the Catholic Church gives us our definition of intercessory prayer:

> "2634. Intercession is a prayer of petition which leads us to pray *as Jesus did*. He is the one intercessor with the Father on behalf of all men, especially sinners. (Romans 8:34; 1 John 2: 1; 1 Timothy 2: 5-8) He is "able for all time to save those who draw near to God through him, since he always lives to make intercession for them" (Hebrews 7: 25)

---

and the Coronation of Mary.

122 *Catechism of the Catholic Church*, 2708.

The Holy Spirit "himself intercedes for us… and intercedes for the saints according to the will of God." (Romans 8: 26-27)

"2635. Since Abraham, intercession—asking on behalf of another—has been characteristic of a heart attuned to God's mercy. In the age of the Church, Christian intercession participates in Christ's, as an expression of the communion of saints. In intercession, he who prays looks "not only to his own interests, but also to the interest of others," even to the point of praying for those who do him harm. (Phil 2: 4, Acts 7: 60; Luke 23: 38, 34)" [123]

Notice how Sr. Faustina refers to her prayer that stopped the angel, the executor of Divine Wrath! Sr. Faustina describes it this way:

"…I found myself pleading with God for the world with words heard interiorly." [124]

She says, *"pleading with God…"* That is intercession. Is this *not a heart attuned to God's mercy* that looks not to her own sins (her interest) but the sins of the whole world? Is this not the Catechism's definition of Intercessory Prayer?

In order to begin to say the Chaplet of Divine Mercy, *one begins with faith already built up.* Therefore, the Chaplet, an intercessory type of prayer, does not begin with the *Apostles Creed*, but the *Our Father*, the Community Prayer of Christians. And since as the Catechism's definition of Intercessory Prayer states *"Intercession is a prayer of petition which leads us to pray as Jesus did…"* we, therefore, begin as Jesus taught us, with the *Our Father*.

Intercession also involves an expression of the Communion of Saints. Therefore we go to the *Hail Mary* to involve our Mother. Our Mother can call upon legions of prayer warriors for our support. She is the Queen of Heaven and Earth, of the Church Triumphant, the Church Suffering, and the Church Militant; Queen of the saints in heaven, in purgatory and on earth: Queen of the communion of Saints. On earth she is honored by all those who pray the rosary, e.g., The Blue Army, the Legion of Mary, the World Apostolate of Fatima, the Cenacle of Priests, Opus Dei, Medjugorje Prayer Groups, just to name a few.

Once we have taken these steps in our intercessory prayer we reinforce or bolster our position by stating who we are by what we believe, as outlined in the *Apostles Creed*.

---

123 *Ibid.*, 2634 and 2635
124 Diary Entry 474

As we can see, the Chaplet is similar to the Rosary in its prayers, but not in order, since it is a different form of prayer: *Intercession and not meditation.*

The Chaplet at the beginning of its decades has a *"Jesus directed"* prayer that goes to the heart of the entire plan of Divine Mercy. That prayer is the one presented in Diary Entry 475 and given its position in the chaplet in Diary Entry 476.

"...Eternal Father, I offer You the Body and Blood, Soul and Divinity of Your dearly beloved Son, Our Lord Jesus Christ, in atonement for our sins and those of the whole world..."

This prayer given to us by Jesus is the summation of His entire ministry of intercession for us. By giving us this prayer He has commissioned us to be His ambassadors so that we can do exactly what He continues to do before the Father in heaven. We find His intercessory mission in the Epistle to the Hebrews

"It follows, then, that his power to save those who come to God through him is absolute, since he lives for ever to intercede for them." [125]

This continuing of the Priesthood of Jesus Christ through the ordained priests, the ministerial or sacerdotal priesthood, is expressed very beautifully by the Catechism *when it quotes* the Council of Trent:

"The Eucharist is thus a sacrifice because it *re-presents* (makes present) the sacrifice of the cross, because it is its *memorial* and because it *applies* its fruits:
'[Christ], our Lord and God, was once and for all to offer himself to God the Father by his death on the altar of the cross, to accomplish there an everlasting redemption. *But because his priesthood was not to end with his death*, at the Last Supper 'on the night when he was betrayed,' [he wanted] to leave to his beloved spouse the Church a visible sacrifice (as the nature of man demands) by which the bloody sacrifice which he was to accomplish once for all on the cross would be re-presented, its memory perpetuated until the end of the world, *and its salutary power be applied to the forgiveness of sins we daily commit.*' (Trent: DS 1743)" [126]

---

125 Hebrews 7: 25
126 *Catechism of the Catholic Church*, 1366

When we are baptized we are anointed with two oils: On our breastplate, the oil of the Catechumens, a healing and strengthening oil, and on our forehead, the Oil of Chrism used for the ordination of priests and bishops. With Chrism we are anointed into the Priesthood, Prophet-hood and Kingship of Jesus, as it says in the Catechism:

> "Christ, high priest and unique mediator, has made of the Church 'a kingdom, priests for his God and Father (1 Peter 2: 5, 9).' The whole community of believers is, as such, priestly. The faithful exercise their baptismal priesthood through their participation, each according to his own vocation, in Christ's mission as priest, prophet, and king. Through the sacraments of Baptism and Confirmation the faithful are 'consecrated to be…a holy priesthood.' (*Lumen Gentium* 10 – 1)" [127]

Since the Catechism refers back to *Lumen Gentium*, the Vatican II document on the Church, it is appropriate to quote that document:

> "Though they differ from one another in essence and not only degree, the common priesthood of the faithful and the ministerial or hierarchical priesthood are nonetheless interrelated. Each of them in its own special way is a participation in the one priesthood of Christ. The ministerial priest, by the sacred power he enjoys, molds and rules the priestly people. Acting in the person of Christ, he brings about the Eucharistic Sacrifice, and offers it to God in the name of all the people. For their part, the faithful join in the offering of the Eucharist by virtue of their royal priesthood, they likewise exercise that priesthood by receiving the sacraments, by praying and thanksgiving, by witness of a holy life, and by self-denial and active charity." [128]

With Jesus' direction to pray this prayer at the beginning of each decade of the Chaplet, we fulfill what Vatican II quoted from what our First Pope wrote in the first papal encyclical:

> "He is the living stone, rejected by human beings but chosen by God and precious to him; set yourselves close to him so that you, too, may be living stones making a spiritual house as a holy priesthood to offer the spiritual sacrifices made acceptable to God through Jesus Christ." [129]

---

127   *Ibid.*, 1546
128   *Lumen Gentium*, article 10, paragraph 2
129   1 Peter 2: 4-5

This prayer of the Chaplet that Jesus has given us to say:

"Eternal Father, I offer You the Body and Blood, Soul and Divinity of Your dearly beloved Son, Our Lord Jesus Christ, in atonement for our sins and those of the whole world." [130]

not only gives us the power to act as an intercessor, participating in praying as He does, but also to act out our common priesthood, the priesthood which we all share in Jesus Christ by Baptism.

The Chaplet, therefore, is an extension of the offering of the Eucharist by the Priest in Mass since the words "Body and Blood, Soul and Divinity," as the Catechism of the Council of Trent states, in its *CANONS ON THE MOST HOLY SACRAMENT OF THE EUCHARIST— 13th Session, Canon 1.* as it describes the presence of the Lord Jesus in the Eucharist:

> "Canon 1. If anyone denies that in the sacrament of the most Holy Eucharist are contained truly, really and substantially the body and blood together with the soul and divinity of our Lord Jesus Christ, and consequently the whole Christ, but says that He is in it only as in a sign, or figure or force, let him be anathema."

Offering this prayer to the Father by direction of Jesus Christ we can extend the benefits of the Eucharist to every moment of existence, fulfilling what Vatican Council II asks us to do:

> "The Church, therefore, earnestly desires that Christ's faithful, when present at this mystery of faith, should not be there as strangers or silent spectators. On the contrary, through a proper appreciation of the rites and prayers they should participate knowingly, devoutly, and actively. They should be instructed by God's word and be refreshed at the table of the Lord's body; they should give thanks to God; by offering the Immaculate Victim, not only through the hands of the priests, but also with him, they should learn to offer themselves too. Through Christ the Mediator, they should be drawn day by day into ever closer union with God and with each other, so that finally God may be all in all." [131]

Father George Kosicki writing about this Chaplet prayer said:

---

130 Diary Entry 475
131 *Document on the Liturgy,* article 48

"By this Eucharistic offering we can unite ourselves with Christ present now in all the tabernacles of the world." [132]

His statement leads into another relationship between the Rosary and the Chaplet of Divine Mercy. Before Our Lady appeared to the children of Fatima, the Guardian Angel of Portugal appeared to them three times. On the third and final apparition he appeared holding a chalice with a host suspended above it. From the host, drops of blood fell into the chalice. Leaving the Chalice and Host suspended in mid-air, he prostrated himself upon the ground and three times repeated this sublime prayer of adoration and reparation:

"Most Holy Trinity, Father, Son and Holy Ghost, I adore You profoundly and I offer You the most precious Body, Blood, Soul and Divinity of Jesus Christ, present in all the tabernacles of the world, in reparation for the outrages, sacrileges and indifference by which He Himself is offended. And by the infinite merits of His Most Sacred Heart and the Immaculate Heart of Mary, I beg of You the conversion of poor sinners." [133]

The similarities to the chief prayer of the Chaplet of Divine Mercy are obvious.

The differences are profound!

Here an angel is offering the prayer. No matter how much the angel would desire to do so, the angel *cannot* and *does not* participate in the Priesthood of Jesus. Therefore, the angel addresses the prayer to the Trinity. Since we participate in the priesthood of Jesus we offer the prayer to the Father, with Jesus.

The angel's prayer speaks of reparation for offenses against the Real Presence in its *reserved* form in the Tabernacle: a very narrow threshold of sins, however horrendous.

The prayer of the Chaplet speaks of atonement for *all sins*, not just offenses against the Eucharistic Presence.

The prayer of the angel continues with a request that the infinite merits of the Sacred Heart of Jesus and the Immaculate Heart of Mary gain the conversion of sinners. The linkage of Mary with Jesus for the conversion of sinners is proper as the initial step to the fullness of Divine Mercy. But the

---

132 Fr. George Kosicki, *Now is the Time for Mercy* (Stockbridge, MA: Marian Helpers, 1993) p. 75.

133 Msgr. William C. McGrath, "The Lady of the Rosary," in *A Woman Clothed With the Sun*, (Garden City, NY: Image Books, 1960) p. 180.

application of Divine Mercy can only come through the infinite merits of Jesus Christ alone.

We might be invited through the Love of God to be a victim soul and participate in the Passion and Death of Jesus Christ, but this is a privilege extended by God and in no way adds any additional merit to the total, complete and perfect sacrifice of Jesus Christ.

This is summed up in the final words of the prayer of the Chaplet:

"...in atonement for our sins and those of the whole world."

In our intercession with Jesus Christ we attest to the words of St. John:

"He is the sacrifice to expiate our sins, and not only ours, but also those of the whole world." [134]

In the Rosary, we go next to the ten Hail Mary's, asking Mary to join us in prayer and keep us focused on the mysteries of the Life of Jesus Christ.

But in the Chaplet we continue our *intercessory* role and keep our focus on the Passion of the Lord by saying the following prayer *on* the *"Hail Mary"* beads:

"For the sake of His sorrowful Passion have mercy on us and on the whole world."

The final prayer *"Holy God. Holy Mighty One. Holy Immortal One,"* is *The Trisagion*, a hymn used in the liturgy of the Byzantine rite, chosen by Jesus to close the Chaplet of Divine Mercy. It is most fascinating, since Jesus crosses liturgical lines and uses the great doxology of the Byzantine Church.

In fact, it is part of our liturgy for Good Friday finding it lifted directly into the "Reproaches" themselves. My old *The New Saint Joseph Daily Missal* published in 1959, from which the first reproach, as my example, gives the response in both Greek and Latin and then English:

"1 and 2 O My people, what Have I done to you, or in what have I offended you? Answer me.
V. Because I led you out of the land of Egypt, you have prepared a Cross for your Savior.
1. *Agios, o Theos!* 2. *Sanctus Deus!* (O Holy God!)
1. *Agios ischyros!* 2. *Sanctus Fortis!* (O Holy Strong One!)

---

134 1 John 2: 2

1. *Agios Athanatos, Eleison imas. 2. Sanctus immortalis, miserere nobis* (O Holy, Immortal One, have mercy on us.)" [135]

Father George Kosicki explains this very well:

"The Father is *the Holy God*, and Father of all. The Son is *the Mighty One* who saved us and did the works of the Father by the power of the Holy Spirit. The Holy Spirit, *the Immortal One*, is the Ever-living Lord God, "the Giver of Life' (Nicene Creed). [136]

This concluding prayer of the chaplet echoes Sacred Scripture from the prophet Isaiah: *"Holy, Holy, Holy, is the Lord of Hosts; the whole earth is full of His glory" (Is 6: 3);* and again, *"For thus says he who is high and exalted, living eternally, whose name is the Holy One" (Is 57: 15);* and the prophet Habakkuk: *"Are you not from eternity, O Lord, my holy God, Immortal?" (Habakkuk 1: 12)"* [137]

Not only is it our duty to pray the Chaplet of Divine Mercy, it is our privilege to participate in the intercessory prayer of Jesus and extend the Eucharistic Prayer of Jesus, the High Priest, to the entire world of our brothers and sisters,

This Chaplet contains within itself a power that can only be found in the Blood of Jesus Christ as Sr. Faustina says:

"Never before had I prayed with such inner power as I did then." [138]

The Father tells St. Faustina about this power:

"When I entered my solitude, I heard these words: **At the hour of their death, I defend as My own glory every soul that will say this chaplet; or when others say it for a dying person, indulgence is the same. When (205) this chaplet is said by the beside of a dying person, God's anger is placated, unfathomable mercy envelops the soul, and the very depths of My tender mercy are moved for the sake of the sorrowful Passion of My Son.**

---

135 *The New Saint Joseph Missal* (The Catholic Book Publishing Company: New York, 1959) p. 332
136 Kosicki, *op. cit.*, pp. 77-8
137 *Ibid.*
138 Diary Entry 474

Oh if only everyone realized how great the Lord's mercy is and how much we all need that mercy, especially at that crucial hour!" [139]

and:

"Once, as I was going down the hall to the kitchen, I heard these words in my soul: **Say unceasingly the chaplet that I have taught you. Whoever will recite it will receive great mercy at the hour of death. Priests will recommend it to sinners as their last hope of salvation. Even if there were a sinner most hardened, if he were to recite this chaplet only once, he would receive grace from My infinite mercy. I desire that the whole world know My infinite mercy. I desire to grant unimaginable graces to those souls who trust in My mercy.**" [140]

Even though I understand all this now, I found new information that explains the still *greater* power of this prayer.

The Diary also gives us the important event for which Jesus taught this Chaplet prayer to Sr. Faustina. The circumstances of this event give us an understanding of the full power of the prayer itself: a power beyond our wildest imagination and a prayer really made for today's times.

"In the evening, when I was in my cell, I saw an Angel, the executor of divine wrath. He was clothed in a dazzling robe, his face gloriously bright, a cloud beneath his feet. from the cloud, bolts of thunder and flashes of lightning were springing into his hands; and from his hand they were going forth, and only then were they striking the earth. When I saw this sign of divine wrath which was about to strike the earth, and in particular a certain place, which for good reasons I cannot name, I began to implore the Angel to hold off for a few moments, and the world would do penance. But my plea was a mere nothing in the face of the divine anger.

Just then I saw the Most Holy Trinity. The greatness of Its majesty pierced me deeply, and I did not dare to repeat my entreaties. At that very moment I felt in my soul the power of Jesus' grace, which dwells in my soul. When I became conscious of this grace, I was instantly snatched up before the Throne of God. Oh, how great is our Lord and God and how incomprehensible His holiness! I will make no attempt

---

139   *Ibid.*, Entry 811
140   *Ibid.*, Entry 687

to describe this greatness, because before long we shall all see Him as He is. I found myself pleading with (197) God for the world with words heard interiorly.

As I was praying in this manner, I saw the Angel's helplessness: he could not carry out the just punishment which was rightly due for sins. Never before had I prayed with such inner power as I did then." [141]

This entry shows that the prayer which begins each decade *and* was taught by Jesus Himself, is imbued with a *power that holds back the just punishment of God rightly due our sins.*

Wouldn't you like to know what sin caused this Divine Wrath? And what city was spared?

You will *NOT* find it in the Diary.

However, Blessed Fr. Michael Sopocko, Sr. Faustina's spiritual director asked those questions and we have found the answers in his writings. What is the crime that caused the Divine Wrath? Fr. Michael Sopocko writes:

"She wrote in her diary that Jesus Himself said that He was about to destroy one of the most beautiful cities of our country like Sodom (was destroyed) on account of the crimes perpetrated there. Having read about these things in the Diary I asked her what does this prophecy mean? She answered confirming what she wrote and replying to a further question of mine, on account of what kind of sins God was going to inflict these punishments. She answered especially for the killing of infants not yet born, the most grievous crime of all." [142]

Sister Faustina herself talks about the pains she suffered for those mothers who were aborting their children.

"September 16, 1937. I wanted very much to make a Holy Hour before the Blessed Sacrament today, but God's will was otherwise. At eight o'clock I was seized with such violent pains that (31) I had to go to bed at once. I was convulsed with pain for three hours; that is, until eleven o'clock at night. No medicine had any effect on me, and whatever I swallowed I threw up. At times, the pains caused me to lose

---

141 *Ibid.*, 474

142 Michael Sopocko, The "Summarium," p. 95, No. 251, in transcripts faxed to Life Foundation Ministries from the National Shrine of Divine Mercy, Stockbridge, MA 03/15/97 from Fr. Seraphim Michalenko, Vice Postulator of the Canonization of Blessed Faustina Kowalska.

consciousness. Jesus had me realize that in this way I took part in His Agony in the Garden, and that He himself allowed these sufferings in order to offer reparation to God for the souls murdered in the wombs of wicked mothers. I have gone through these sufferings three times now. They always start at eight o'clock in the evening and last until eleven. No medicine can lessen these sufferings. When eleven o'clock comes, they cease by themselves, and I fall asleep at that moment. The following day, I feel very weak…" [143]

The city is later identified by Fr. Michael Sopocko and is quoted by Fr. Seraphim Michalenko in an article published in 1995:

"Her confessor later discovered that, between the first and second World Wars, the city of Warsaw, which as the capital of Poland, was also one of the great capitals of abortion in the world! While Sister Faustina lived and prayed, that city was spared. But, hardly a year after her death, Poland was invaded, and by the time the war was over, Warsaw was almost completely destroyed." [144]

Now that we know the origins, meanings and power of the Rosary and the Chaplet of Divine Mercy how do we use these prayers?

I urge you to pray the Rosary to build up your faith as Sister Lucia of Fatima says, by meditating on the Life, Passion, Death and Resurrection of Jesus Christ through the eyes of His Mother, Mary.

Then, once your faith is strengthened, pray the Chaplet of Divine Mercy with its prayers dictated by Jesus Christ, and prayed by Sister Faustina for the first time to hold back the Divine Wrath of His Father against a city whose crimes were *the killing of infants not yet born, the most grievous crime of all.*

It is your right and privilege to participate in the Intercessory Role of Jesus Christ by your Baptism into His Priesthood. By doing so, you extend the Merits of His Holy Sacrifice on the Altar anytime of the day from any place you might be.

We have on this one instrument, the rosary beads, two most powerful weapons in our Spiritual Warfare in these last days of Divine Mercy. We have the Rosary and the Chaplet of Divine Mercy.

Don't leave home without your Rosary beads.

---

143   Diary Entry 1276
144   Fr. Seraphim Michalenko, "The Wombs of Mercy," The Association of Marian Helpers Bulletin, Summer 1995, p. 13.

Chapter 5
The Image of Divine Mercy

Introduction to Chapter 5
The Image of Divine Mercy

The first major talk I gave on the Image of Divine Mercy was after The John Paul II Institute of Divine Mercy's *"An Ocean of Mercy"* Seminar in Houston in 1999. My research into the Diary led me to focus exclusively on what was to become known to me as "The Original Vilnius Image of Divine Mercy." Up to this time I had one of the Hyla images as my personal choice.

In 2001, my wife, Penny, and I were invited by Dr. Robert Stackpole to be seminar teachers and leaders on the John Paul II Institute of Divine Mercy's "Divine Mercy On-Site Seminar to Poland and Lithuania." On that On-Site seminar two incidents happened that changed my thoughts about "The Original Vilnius Image of Divine Mercy."

The first was our visit to Plock and the Sisters Convent where St. Faustina had her first vision of the Divine Mercy. [145] After visiting the present day convent we began to walk the grounds. We came to the original wooden building in which St. Faustina had her cell and received the vision and command to paint an Image of Jesus. Suddenly, out of nowhere, a young sister appeared and asked us whether we would like to go into the old building. Of course, we said yes and Fr. Seraphim kept saying: "I have never been in this building."

We eventually made our way to the 2nd floor and the front room which was the actual place where St. Faustina had her vision. As I stood on the exact spot I sensed that I was to "write" about this Image.

The second was visit to Vilnius, Lithuania. After settling in our hotel we went immediately to the Holy Spirit Church where the Original Vilnius

---

145 Diary Entry 47 and FN 1.

Image of Divine Mercy was enshrined over a side altar. Here we had Mass and Fr. Seraphim asked me to do the lectionary readings.

It was an indescribable experience to have stood in the spot where St. Faustina had her first vision of the Image and then to not only see the actual painting but then to stand in front of it and proclaim the Word of God.

After Mass I visited the gift shop and bought the next to the last copy of the painting which is a cherished memento of our visit.

The Image of Divine Mercy

On February 22, 1931, while staying at Plock, Sister Faustina received an *order* from Jesus to paint an image according to the pattern which He presented her in a vision:

> "In the evening, when I was in my cell, I saw the Lord Jesus clothed in a white garment. One hand [was] raised in the gesture of blessing, the other was touching the garment at the breast. From beneath the garment, slightly drawn aside at the breast, there were emanating two large rays, one red, the other pale. In silence I kept my gaze fixed on the Lord; my soul was struck with awe, but also with great joy. After a while, Jesus said to me, **Paint an image according to the pattern you see, with the signature: Jesus, I trust in You. I desire that this image be venerated, first in your chapel, and [then] throughout the world.**" [146]

We must conclude that this was a *physical* apparition and *not* an interior vision since in the Archives of Sister Faustina we have the recollection of Sister Christine which states:

> "'Children from the town stood in the street opposite the rooms of the nuns and saw rays coming from one of the windows. This was the window of Sister Faustina's cell.'" [147]

What we know about this Image of Divine Mercy is gleaned not just from Sr. Faustina's Diary, but also from historical records of the Congregation, and

---

146   Diary Entry 47
147   Tarnawska, *op.cit.*, p. 116.

in the writings of Reverend Michael Sopocko, one of Sr. Faustina's spiritual directors.

> "...The Servant of God tried to fulfill the command, but not knowing painting techniques, she was unable to do it by herself. Still, she did not give up the idea. She kept returning to it and sought help from other sisters and from her confessors.

> A few years later her superiors sent her to Vilnius (Wilno), where her confessor, Rev. Prof. Michael Sopocko, interested to see *what the picture of a hitherto unknown theme would look like*, asked the painter Eugene Kazimierowski to paint the picture according to Sister Faustina's directions. The picture was finished in June 1934 and hung in the corridor of the Bernardine Sisters' convent near St. Michael's Church in Vilnius, where Father Sopocko was rector..." [148]

It was Fr. Sopocko's interest in *"what the picture of a hitherto unknown theme would look like,"* which caused him to become the instrument by which the Vilnius Image of Divine Mercy [149] was painted and first publicly venerated from the Ostra Brama Gate of the city of Vilnius. We must note that of the confessors and spiritual directors that Sr. Faustina had, only Fr. Michael Sopocko responded to Jesus' request as a personal mission. He applied his knowledge of theology, energy, pastoral influence and, toward the end, his personal finances to it.

Before we begin to study the artistic, thematic and theological meanings of the Vilnius Image of Divine Mercy it is important that we establish that Jesus really wanted this Image to be painted in a *definitive representation*. (See Father Andrasz' comment below – footnote 154)

The first vision that Sr. Faustina received establishes the criteria for the Image of Divine Mercy that Jesus wanted. Jesus said: "*...**Paint an image according to the** pattern **you see...**" [150]

If we understand from scripture that God does not change: *"No, I, Yahweh, do not change...,"* [151] then when God speaks of a *"pattern"* we should pay attention. When Yahweh wants Moses to build a Tent of Meeting God says to him:

---

148 Diary Footnote #1
149 It is called *The Vilnius Image of Divine Mercy* to differentiate from other
      images painted *later* that St. Faustina *never* saw.
150 Diary Entry 47
151 Malachi 3: 6

"This Dwelling and all its furnishings you shall make exactly according to the *pattern* that I will now show you." [152]

and in Exodus 25:

"See that you make them according to the *pattern* shown you on the mountain." [153]

Fourteen (14) times the word "pattern" is used in the Scriptures. 12 times it is used when someone is told to make something that God directs to be made; specifically, Moses' Tent of Meeting, the Temple of David and Solomon.

Therefore, when Sr. Faustina is told "...*Paint an image according to the pattern you see...*," it is important to understand that the only person who ever saw this pattern was Sr. Faustina. To emphasize that the pattern Sr. Faustina sees is the one that Jesus wants, Sr. Faustina reports that Jesus appeared to her 20 more times in the same manner or pattern.

One of her confessors, Fr. Joseph Andrasz, S.J., says:

"The vision of the Merciful Jesus in this particular representation occurred repeatedly during Sister Faustina's lifetime. Our Savior evidently wanted the image to be deeply impressed upon her soul." [154]

Sr. Faustina understood her mission and its urgency. First, she tried to paint it herself although she had no training or artistic skills. [155] When Eugene Kazimierowski was selected to paint the Image, Sr. Faustina's demands concerning the details of the painting frustrated the artist according to Fr. Sopocko.

The Superior at that time, Mother Irene, has this recollection:

"...with my knowledge Father Sopocko looked for an artist who would paint the image of the Merciful Jesus in the manner in which He appeared to Sister Faustina in Plock. Prof. Eugeniusz Kazimierowski undertook to paint the picture. In order not to alert the sisters to the interior experiences of Sister Faustina, every Saturday morning I went

---

152 Exodus 25: 9
153 Exodus 25: 40
154 Joseph Andrasz, S.J., *Divine Mercy... We Trust in You!* (Stockbridge, MA: Marian Helpers, 1986), p. 24.
155 Diary, Footnote 1.

with her to Holy Mass at the Ostra Brama Gate, and after Mass we would go to the painter, to whom Sister Faustina would give exact details as to how he was to paint the picture of the Merciful Jesus. The painter tried assiduously to adapt himself to all Sister Faustina's requirements." [156]

Sister Juliana heard Fr. Sopocko at a conference in May 1940, at St. Michael's Church in Vilnius, and wrote:

"...The difficulties with getting the painting done were great; the artist searched out by Fr. Sopocko, constantly had to keep *repainting the face*, because Sr. Faustina did not want to accept the finished product... After repeated modifications, and exasperations on the part of the artists and the priest, Sr. Faustina, unsatisfied to the end, maintaining that the image is ugly, came and said that the Lord Jesus said to leave the image in the state it's in: *'It isn't good, but it's good enough; it doesn't need to be redone anymore."* [157]

Fr. Michael Sopocko wrote in some notes dated November 25, 1958 while at Bialystosk:

"Upon my request Mr. Eugene Kazimierowski began the painting of the image on January 2, 1934. Sister Faustina of blessed memory with the permission of the Superior, Mother Irene, came once and twice a week to the painter's studio (in the company of another sister) and imparted instructions, how this image is to look. For several months the painter was unable to satisfy the author, who became sad on that account... Mr. Kazimierowski finally asked me, that I help him discharge this task and for a few days pose dressed in an alb with a cincture around the waist. This made it easier for the painter after six months to paint the image, with which Sister Faustina was on the whole satisfied, and she no longer complained about its incorrectness."[158]

---

156 Maria Tarnawska, *op. cit.*, pp. 162-163.

157 Michael Sopocko, Transcripts faxed to Life Foundation Ministries from the National Shrine of Divine Mercy, Stockbridge, MA, 03/15/97 from Fr. Seraphim Michalenko, Vice Postulator of the Canonization of Blessed Faustina Kowalska.

158 Fr. Michael Sopocko, "The Matter of Correctness of the Image of Divine Mercy," *Pillars of Fire in My Soul* (Stockbridge, MA: Marian Press, 2003) p. 83-4.

The *only* person who can state that the painted Image of Divine Mercy is what Jesus wanted is Sr. Faustina. Fr. Sopocko was present at each painting session and heard St. Faustina's directions and comments and has written about many of them in his own writings.

We know that Sr. Faustina thought the painted Image ugly since it failed to convey the beauty of Jesus. But she accepts it because Jesus told her to do so.

There are many other renditions of the Image of Divine Mercy. However, it becomes very important to note that the *only*, and I emphasize, the *only* Image of Divine Mercy that Sr. Faustina ever saw completed was the Vilnius Image of Divine Mercy. It was painted by Eugene Kazimierowski with her personal directions given to the artist during her weekly visits to him.

The Vilnius Image is the only Image of Divine Mercy made according to the *"pattern"* Jesus showed to Sr. Faustina. It is literally, *the only portrait Jesus ever commissioned to be painted*. And Sr. Faustina is the only agent consigned the mission to make sure it was painted. (See the Addendum which follows this chapter.)

The first rendition painted *without* the personal direction of Sr. Faustina was the Stanley Bartowski image placed in the Warsaw Community Chapel in 1943. It should be noted that his first rendition burned during the Warsaw uprising. A second rendition by Bartowski was commissioned by the community. However,

> "In the meantime, the superior of the Cracow house had been approached by the painter Adolf Hyla, who offered to paint some sort of picture for the sisters' chapel as a votive offering for having survived the war... The image was finished in Autumn of 1943 and brought to the Cracow house. Batowski's image arrived at the same time. For this reason a problem arose-which of the images should be kept in the sisters' chapel? It was settled by Cardinal Sapieha, who by chance happened to be present there. He inspected the two pictures and said, "Since Hyla has painted his picture as a votive offering, that picture should stay in the sisters' chapel." ...To this day the picture remains in the side altar to the left of the main entrance, in the Chapel of the Congregation of the Sisters of Our Lady of Mercy at No. 3/9 Wronia Street in Cracow..." [159]

We will discuss this Hyla rendition later. However, please note that both of these renditions were painted around 1943, five (5) years after Sr. Faustina's

159 Diary, Footnote 1

death. *Sister Faustina never saw them! And she is the only one that knew the pattern Jesus wanted painted.*

Artistically, the Vilnius Image of Divine Mercy would be judged mediocre. Fr. Sopocko, who chose the artist, had this to say about his ability:

"Kazimierowski was not a great painter, but he lived in my neighbourhood, I knew him and therefore I turned to him." [160]

and later Fr. Sopocko adds:

"I admit that the picture did not please me greatly from the artistic standpoint." [161]

St. Faustina was less than pleased with the artist's painting and writes:

"Once, when I was visiting the artist [Eugene Kazimierowski] who was painting the image, and saw that it was not as beautiful as Jesus is, I felt very sad about it, but I hid this deep in my heart. When we had left the artist's house, Mother Superior [Irene] stayed in town to attend to some matters while I returned home alone. I went immediately to the chapel and wept a good deal. I said to the Lord, "Who will paint You as beautiful as You are?" Then I heard these words: **Not in the beauty of the color, nor of the brush lies the greatness of this image, but in My grace.**" [162]

And we know Jesus was not full of praise for the artist's ability either from the entry quoted earlier:

"...the Lord Jesus said to leave the image in the state it's in: *'It isn't good, but it's good enough; it doesn't need to be redone anymore.'*" [163]

Since the painting is obviously not an artistic masterpiece, there must be other aspects of it that satisfy Jesus' demand that it be venerated.

160 Maria Tarnawska, *op. cit.*, p163.
161 *Ibid.* p. 165.
162 Diary Entry 313.
163 Michael Sopocko, Transcripts faxed to Life Foundation Ministries from the National Shrine of Divine Mercy, Stockbridge, MA, 03/15/97 from Fr. Seraphim Michalenko, Vice Postulator of the Canonization of Blessed Faustina Kowalska.

"... I desire that this image be venerated, first in your chapel, and [then] throughout the world." [164]

Let us look at the Vilnius Image of Divine Mercy for its thematic and theological aspects. Since this Image is a representation of Jesus to be made according to a specific pattern, it is essentially a Sacred Icon to be venerated. Cardinal Ratzinger, the eminent theologian and Prefect of the Vatican Congregation for the Doctrine of the Faith, now Pope Benedict XVI, has to say about icons in his book, *The Spirit of the Liturgy:*

> "Now history becomes sacrament in Christ, who is the source of the Sacraments. Therefore, the icon of Christ is the center of sacred iconography. The center of the icon of Christ is the Pascal Mystery: Christ is presented as the Crucified, the risen Lord, the One who will come again and who here and now hiddenly reigns over all. Every image of Christ must contain these three essential aspects of the mystery of Christ and, in this sense, must be an image of Easter. ... And, centered as it is on the Paschal Mystery, the image of Christ is always an icon of the Eucharist, that is, it points to the sacramental presence of the Easter mystery. [165]

Let us see if the Vilnius Image of Divine Mercy as a commissioned [166] portrait of Jesus, Himself, fulfills the criteria listed by Cardinal Ratzinger, now Pope Benedict XVI.

First, it must have a reference to the Sacraments, especially Baptism and the Eucharist. When Fr. Sopocko wanted to know what the two rays in the Image represented Sr. Faustina could not answer, so he told her to ask Jesus. This is the response of Jesus:

> "When, on one occasion, my confessor told me to ask the Lord Jesus the meaning of the two rays in the image, I answered, "Very well, I will ask the Lord." During prayer I heard these words within me: **The two rays denote Blood and Water. The pale ray stands for the Water**

---

164 Diary Entry 47.

165 Joseph Cardinal Ratzinger, *The Spirit of the Liturgy*, (San Francisco, CA: Ignatius Press, 2000) pp. 132-3.

166 *"Commission," The American Heritage Dictionary*: "1. The act of committing or giving authority to carry out a particular task or duty, or granting certain powers; and entrusting. 2. The authority so granted. 3. The matter or task as committed..."

which makes souls righteous. The red ray stands for the Blood which is the life of souls...

These two rays issued forth from the very depths of My tender mercy when My agonized Heart was opened by a lance on the Cross..." [167]

Jesus in His answer gives reference to two Sacraments: The Eucharist, since it *re-presents* the *"offering of the body of Jesus Christ made once and for all."* [168] Jesus pinpoints that moment when He says: ***"These two rays issued forth from the very depths of My tender mercy when My agonized Heart was opened by a lance on the Cross."***

The Sacrament of the Eucharist is *"the source and summit of all Christian Life,"* [169] to include each sacrament, then *"The pale ray stands for the Water which makes souls righteous"* alludes to the Sacrament of Baptism by whose waters we are made righteous. *"The red ray stands for the Blood which is the life of souls..."* which is the Eucharist since Jesus says:

"In all truth I tell you, if you do not eat the flesh of the Son of Man and drink his blood, you have no life in you." [170]

Additionally, Fr. Sopocko tells us that it also represents the Sacrament of Penance.

"The Image should represent Christ at the moment of instituting the sacrament of penance with the words 'Peace to You!', the right hand at the height of the shoulder, the eyes directed downward; the whole figure frontally expresses and bestows peace; the rays should be directed towards the onlooker, and towards the ground. The background (should be) dark or (there should be the) doors of the Cenacle..." [171]

Second, the Vilnius Image of Divine Mercy does show Jesus as the Crucified Christ and He, in His own words to Sr. Faustina validates this. If you study the Image carefully you notice that Jesus is looking downward and not straight out in the usual portrait style. Sr. Faustina writes in Diary Entry 326:

---

167 Diary, Entry 299.
168 Hebrews 10: 10
169 *Catechism of the Catholic Church*, 1324.
170 John 6: 53
171 Michael Sopocko, quoted in *Pillars of Fire in My Soul*, pp. 82-3.

"Once, Jesus said to me, **My gaze from this image is like My gaze from the cross.**" [172]

and also (quoted above):

"**...These two rays issued forth from the very depths of My tender mercy when My agonized Heart was opened by a lance on the Cross.**" [173]

Third, the Vilnius Image also shows the Risen Christ. Fr. Sopocko says: "The Image should represent Christ at the moment of instituting the sacrament of Penance with the words 'Peace to You!' the right hand at the height of the shoulder, the eyes directed downward; the whole figure frontally expresses and bestows peace; the rays should be directed towards the onlooker, and towards the ground. The background (should be) dark or (there should be the) doors of the Cenacle..." [174]

The Cenacle reference is to Easter Sunday evening when Jesus enters the Upper Room and appears to the Apostles, and according to the Gospel of John institutes the Sacrament of Penance. [175] Jesus is very much alive as Fr. Sopocko continues to explain:

"Regarding the description of the image, according to Sister Faustina the image is to represent the Lord Jesus in a walking posture, clothed in a long white garment with a band (belt?!) round the waist. The eyes must be somewhat cast down, and the look (gaze?) – as from the cross – merciful. With the right hand he's to be blessing the world, and with left – opening (drawing aside) the garment in the area of the two rays: on the right of the onlooker a pale (colorless) one, on the left a red one. These rays are to be transparent, but appropriately throwing light on the figure of the Savior, as well as on the area (space) in front of him." [176]

Fourth, the Vilnius Image of Divine Mercy also presents to us *the One*

---

172   S. Maria Faustina *op. cit.*, Entry 326, p. 148.
173   S. Maria Faustina *op. cit.*, Entry 299, p. 139.
174   Michael Sopocko, *ibid.* pp. 82-3.
175   John 20: 19-23
176   Sopocko, *op.cit.*, p. 81

who will come again and who here and now hiddenly reigns over all." As Jesus through the opening in His Side is revealing the Coming Glory of His Resurrected Body filled with the Heavenly Light. We should recall what Matthew says in his gospel at the time of the Death of Jesus: *"And suddenly, the veil of the Sanctuary was torn in two from top to bottom..."* [177] The pierced Heart of Jesus is torn and His transfigured glory begins to speak of Him who will come to reign, but is still hidden from us.

Now notice in the Vilnius Image of Divine Mercy that Jesus is dressed in a plain white tunic tied at the waist with a cord and He is in His bare feet. Doesn't that seem odd? It should not. Jesus fulfills all the prophecies in the Feast of *Yom Kippur*, the Day of Atonement, by being not only the victim, but also the altar, and *the High Priest* as we read in Hebrews

> "Since in Jesus, the Son of God, we have the supreme high priest who has gone through to the highest heaven, we must hold firm to our profession of faith. [15] For the high priest we have is not incapable of feeling our weaknesses with us, but has been put to the test in exactly the same way as ourselves, apart from sin. [16] Let us, then, have no fear in approaching the throne of grace to receive mercy and to find grace when we are in need of help.

> Every high priest is taken from among human beings and is appointed to act on their behalf in relationships with God, to offer gifts and sacrifices for sins; [2] he can sympathise with those who are ignorant or who have gone astray, because he too is subject to the limitations of weakness. [3] That is why he has to make sin offerings for himself as well as for the people. [4] No one takes this honour on himself; it needs a call from God, as in Aaron's case. [5] And so it was not Christ who gave himself the glory of becoming high priest, but the one who said to him: You are my Son, today I have fathered you, [6] and in another text: You are a priest for ever, of the order of Melchizedek. [7] During his life on earth, he offered up prayer and entreaty, with loud cries and with tears, to the one who had the power to save him from death, and, winning a hearing by his reverence, [8] he learnt obedience, Son though he was, through his sufferings; [9] when he had been perfected, he became for all who obey him the source of eternal salvation [10] and was acclaimed by God with the title of high priest of the order of Melchizedek". [178]

---

177 Matthew 27: 51
178 Hebrews 4: 14-16, 5: 1-10

Only once a year did the High Priest officiate in the Sanctuary, on *Yom Kippur*, the Day of Atonement. On other major feasts when he was present he would be arrayed in his magnificent High Priestly Robes. You can read all the details of the High Priest's magnificent robes in Exodus 39: 1-26. These garments were so glorious that some rabbis wrote that when the sun shone on the High Priest he radiated like the Shekinah Glory of Yahweh.

However, on the Day of Atonement, when only the High Priest officiates, he must take off his magnificent robes and put on a plain tunic of fine linen God prescribed for Aaron and his sons. We read this in Leviticus:

> "'This is how he must enter the sanctuary: with a young bull for a sacrifice for sin and a ram for a burnt offering. [4] He will put on a tunic of consecrated linen, wear linen drawers on his body, a linen waistband round his waist, and a linen turban on his head. These are the sacred vestments he will put on after washing himself." [179]

One the High Priest has completed his duties within the Holy of Holies and the Holy Place he will put aside his sacred linen vestments and robe again in his glorious High Priest vestments:

> "When he has sent the goat into the desert, Aaron will go back into the Tent of Meeting and take off the linen vestments which he wore to enter the sanctuary and leave them there. [24] He will then wash his body inside the holy place, put on his vestments and come outside to offer his own and the people's burnt offering. He will perform the rite of expiation for himself and for the people, [25] and burn the fat of the sacrifice for sin on the altar." [180]

On *Yom Kippur*, the Day of Atonement, two goats are used in the Feast for a sacrifice of sin for the community. [181] One goat chosen by lot was the *scapegoat*. [182] After the High Priest laid hands on its head and transferred the sins of the people to it, it was led into the desert and released. The other goat is sacrificed and its blood used in the sprinkling of the Mercy Seat over the Ark of the Covenant in the Holy of Holies.

---

179 Leviticus 16: 3-4
180 Leviticus 16: 22b - 25
181 Leviticus 16: 5-10, 15-16
182 Leviticus 16: 8, 10, and 26, names this goat "for *Azazel*" since the High Priest has laid hands on him and transferred the sins of the people to it. He is sent into the desert, is not killed, and therefore "scapes."

The High Priest, and only he, would enter the Holy of Holies to sprinkle the blood of the goat on the Mercy Seat over the Ark of the Covenant.

"'The rite of expiation will be performed by the priest who has been anointed and installed to officiate in succession to his father. He will put on the linen vestments, the sacred vestments...'" [183]

This is confirmed by Saint Paul n Hebrews:

"Under these provisions, priests go regularly into the outer tent to carry out their acts of worship, [7] but the second tent is entered only once a year, and then only by the high priest who takes in the blood to make an offering for his own and the people's faults of inadvertence." [184]

Moses had to take off his sandals on the Holy Ground before the Burning Bush. So the High Priest enters barefooted into the *Holy of Holies,* the place where God meets man, the holiest ground of all.

Jesus, the High Priest *and* the Victim, as He exits the Holy of Holies, as you see *in the Image,* He is pointing to His pieced Heart from which emanate two rays representing the blood and water with which He *"sprinkled"* the Mercy Seat in *"the sanctuary not made by human hands"* in Heaven:

"But now Christ has come, as the high priest of all the blessings which were to come. He has passed through the greater, the more perfect tent, not made by human hands, that is, not of this created order; [12] and he has entered the sanctuary once and for all, taking with him not the blood of goats and bull calves, but his own blood, having won an eternal redemption" [185]

Two other points need to be noted. Jesus' right hand is raised in a blessing. The last solemn act of the High Priest on the Day of Atonement was to offer the evening sacrifice of incense on the Golden Altar and then bless the people:

"Then he would come down and raise his hands over the whole assembly of the Israelites to give them the Lord's blessing from his lips, being privileged to pronounce his name" [186]

---

183 Leviticus 16: 32
184 Hebrews 9: 6-7
185 Hebrews 9: 11-12
186 Sirach (Ecclesiasticus) 50: 20

But why is the rest of the Image that is around Jesus so dark?

In the construction and erection notes in 1 Kings we find that the place of the inner most part of the sanctuary, the Holy of Holies, (the *dabir*) (דְּבִר) (deb-eer) (1687), where the Ark of the Covenant with the Mercy Seat is located, is approximately 30 feet by 30 feet by 30 feet. Where the opening would be there was a veil or curtain from top to bottom. [187] No light entered the Holy of Holies. It was totally dark.

The only light came from the Glory of Yahweh that filled it, or as it came to be known, the *Shekinah Glory*. The Glory was so bright it appeared black. It is not unlike the reaction our eyes have after looking directly into the flash of a camera. The brightness appears dark with a faint interior glow.

In the Image of Divine Mercy, Jesus is coming out of the Holy of Holies in Heaven which is filled with the Glory of God. Since he is now resurrected, that Glory is beginning to emanate from the wound in His side. [188]

Before I discuss the other renditions of the Image of Divine Mercy I must relate to you something very important from the Diary of St. Faustina and the writings of Maria Tarnawska in her book, *Sister Faustina Kowalska – Her Life and Mission*.

Anyone who has read the Diary of St. Faustina has been frustrated because it is apparently not written in a normal chronological sequence of diaries. There is a reason for this and we find it, not in the Diary proper, but in the footnotes:

> "That is elsewhere in the diary. For a long time Sister Faustina did not take notes of her experiences and of graces received. It was only at the explicit order of her confessor, Father Sopocko, that she began to write down her experiences as they occurred, and also earlier ones as she remembered them. After some time, she burned her notes. Father Sopocko gives the following account: "When I was in the Holy Land for a few weeks, she was persuaded by a supposed angel to burn the diary. As penance, I told her to reconstruct the part destroyed. But in the meantime new experiences came, and she wrote down new and old things alternately. Hence the lack of chronological order in the diary." [189]

Did the Devil want the Diary destroyed, just because of her spiritual writings or for something specific in the Diary? We would not find out the answer to that question without the wonderful research done by Maria

---

187 1 Kings 6: 15-22
188 Prefigured in Matthew 27: 50-51
189 Diary, Footnote 42

Tarnawska. In her discussion about the destruction of the Diary and its re-construction, Tarnawska wrote:

> "Sadly, the part of her Diary which was destroyed also contained the story of how the Image of Jesus of the Divine Mercy came about, which was written as it happened, for it was at that time that it was painted. Before Sister Faustina returned to writing her diary, the picture was ready. In the new version of her Diary she does not often revert to that theme. Luckily, we have the supplementary account of the then superior, Mother Irene, and of Father Sopocko." [190]

The first part of this quote is worth repeating:

> "Sadly, the part of her Diary which was destroyed also contained the story of how the Image of Jesus of the Divine Mercy came about, which was written as it happened, for it was at that time that it was painted."

Jesus wanted the Image, whose pattern He insisted be followed when painted, to be venerated. Therefore, the Devil had a desire to destroy the knowledge of how, for what reason it was painted.

This also explains why in the reconstructed Diary the very first entry, is a poem about the Image of Divine Mercy.

> "O Eternal Love, You command Your Sacred Image[1] to be painted
> And reveal to us the inconceivable fount of mercy,
> You bless whoever approaches Your rays,
> And a soul all black will turn into snow.
>
> O sweet Jesus, it is here[2] You established the throne of Your mercy
> To bring joy and hope to sinful man.
> From Your open Heart, as from a pure fount,
> Flows comfort to a repentant heart and soul.
>
> May praise and glory for this Image
> Never cease to stream from man's soul.
> May praise of God's mercy pour from every heart,
> Now, and at every hour, and forever and ever.
>
> O My God [191]

---

190 Tarnawska, *op.cit.*, p. 162
191 Diary, Entry 1

Where the poem reads *"O sweet Jesus, it is here You established the throne of Your Mercy,"* Footnote 2 tells where that Throne of Mercy is:

"That is, in the picture. [192]

The conclusion we must draw as to why the Devil wanted the Diary destroyed when he got permission to tempt St. Faustina to do so, was to destroy the important information about why Jesus wanted the Image painted and that it be done according to the pattern He Himself established, because it was to be *"The Throne of His Mercy."*

And even a poor reproduction of the original Vilnius Image carried tremendous power and graces as related by St. Faustina in a letter to Fr. Sopocko on 21st of February 1938:

> "God gave me to know that He is pleased with what has already been done. Immersed in prayer and close to God, I experienced profound peace in my soul concerning this whole work... As regards these holy cards, the situation is not so bad. People have started buying them and many a soul has already obtained God's grace which flows from this source. As with everything else, it goes slowly. These pictures are not as nice as the large painted image. They are being purchased by those who are attracted by God's grace, and it is God Himself who acts here. [193]

This is confirmed by St. Faustina in her Diary when she is given a booklet, *"Christ the King of Mercy"* in which Fr. Sopocko published the Chaplet and Novena with a series of ejaculations from the Diary that he formed into a Litany of the Divine Mercy. Given a copy to review she wrote:

> "When I looked at this image, I was pierced with such a lively love for God that, for a moment, I did not know where I was. When we had finished our business, we went to the Church of the Most Holy Virgin Mary. We attended Holy Mass, during which the Lord gave me to know what a great number of souls would attain salvation through this work. Then I entered into an intimate conversation with the Lord, thanking Him for having condescended to grant me the grace of seeing how the veneration of His unfathomable mercy is spreading..." [194]

---

192 Diary, FN 2.

193 *The Letters of Saint Faustina,* translated by Sr. M. Beata Piekut O.L.M., (Cracow, Poland: Misericordia Publications, 2007), p. 106-8.

194 Diary, Entry 1300

and:

"November 10, [1937]. When Mother [Irene] showed me the booklet with the chaplet, the litany and the novena, I asked her to let me look it over. As I was glancing through it, Jesus gave me to know interiorly: **Already there are many souls who have been drawn to My love by this image. My mercy acts in souls through this work.** I learned that many souls had experienced God's grace." [195]

Keep in mind we are talking copies of the *Original* Vilnius Image, the only Image St. Faustina knew.

Knowing all this, let us discuss the *non*-Vilnius Images.

Earlier I had mentioned that the first rendition painted *without* the personal direction of Sr. Faustina was the Stanley Bartowski image placed in the Warsaw Community Chapel in 1943. It burned during the Warsaw uprising. [196] A second rendition by Bartowski was commissioned by the community, but before it could be installed a painting by Adolf Hyla arrived, was chosen instead and placed in that Chapel. It remains there to this day.

The Hyla is the most popular of all the renditions. *But that does not make it correct according the pattern Jesus wanted His portrait to be painted!* See Fr. Sopocko's comments below!

Fr. Michael Sopocko saw the Hyla image and took immediate offense. His writings concerning it very explicitly and categorically denied it was a correct representation of the "*pattern*" that Jesus directed Sr. Faustina to follow. Here are Fr. Sopocko's comments without embellishment. They are long but because of their importance his comments must be as detailed and complete as possible.

"The Hyla image must have been painted in 1946, since I already found it in 1947 and I ascertained the following deficiencies: blatant feminism – the whole figure is curved (as though dancing); the right hand raised too high, expressing action (drama or comedy), and not composure (serenity); the rays overly materialistic, like ropes; a skittish look directed somewhere into space; an inappropriate background (formerly there were flowers, and now a tile floor and the blue of the sky – no logic)... [197]

---

195 *Ibid.*, Entry 1379
196 Diary, Footnote 1
197 Stackpole, *op. cit.*, p82

When I came (to Cracow) from Wilno (August 1947), I brought to the attention of the Sisters of Our Lady of Mercy that that image does not correspond at all to Sr. Faustina's vision, and I asked Mr. Hyla to correct it and not to paint such images anymore. Unfortunately, Mr. Hyla did not come into line with my observations (remarks) and said point-blank that he is going to paint the kind of images that those commissioning him are going to want, and he executed a couple hundred of them against a variety of backgrounds... [198]

...Mr. Hyla's stubbornness and that of the people who distribute his images is negatively disposing the Bishops, the cause of devotion to The Divine Mercy, and to me, because – as I recently found out – *they impute to me that I not only tolerate this, but even support it*, up to now, in order to avoid conflict, I kept silent, but from now on, *for the good of the cause, I have to tell the truth.* [199]

Recall the earlier quote of Fr. Michael Sopocko's comments about what Jesus said to Sr. Faustina concerning Vilnius Image of Divine Mercy:

"...The difficulties with getting the painting done were great; the artist searched out by Fr. Sopocko, constantly had to keep repainting the face, because Sr. Faustina did not want to accept the finished product... After repeated modifications, and exasperations on the part of the artists and the priest, Sr. Faustina, unsatisfied to the end, maintaining that the image is ugly, came and said that the Lord Jesus said to leave the image in the state it's in: *'It isn't good, but it's good enough; it doesn't need to be redone anymore.'*" [200]

Notice it says *"...the artist searched out by Fr. Sopocko, constantly had to keep repainting the face..."*

As an aside, it is interesting to note that the original Vilnius Image was rolled up and stored behind some furniture during World War II. When it was brought out the *"face"* was horribly damaged and had to be redone.

If Jesus says that *it isn't good, but it's good enough,* what is it good enough for? The answer will surprise you as it did those who discovered it.

In March 1993 a group of lay people banded together under the title Life

198   *Ibid.*, p. 86.
199   *Ibid.*, pp. 87-8.
200   Michael Sopocko, Transcripts faxed to Life Foundation Ministries from the National Shrine of Divine Mercy, Stockbridge, MA, 03/15/97 from Fr. Seraphim Michalenko, Vice Postulator of the Canonization of Blessed Faustina Kowalska.

Foundation Ministries, a Pro-Life Anti-Abortion evangelization outreach under the patronage of Our Lady of Guadalupe. Gradually they came to believe that the Divine Mercy Message and its Devotion needed to be included in their message. To that regard,

> "...January 4th, the Vice-Postulator [for the Cause of Sister Faustina] gave Life Foundation Ministries a negative of a photograph of the first Image of The Divine Mercy which was painted according to Blessed Faustina's instructions, representing the image in its state before the damaged face was touched up prior to its definitive placement in the Church of the Holy Spirit in Vilnius, Lithuania, after the fall of Communism there. Shortly after, prints of the original Divine Mercy Image were made available [by Life Foundation Ministries] in a size suitable for use in homes, primarily to fulfill the Lord's command to Sister Faustina: 'I want it [the image] to be venerated publicly so that every soul may know about [My Mercy]' (Diary, Notebook 1, p 142) and by means of this image I shall be granting many graces to souls; so let every soul have access to it' (Notebook II, p. 40)." [201]

Life Foundation Ministries uses illuminated Images of the Shroud of Turin, Our Lady of Guadalupe and the Vilnius Image of Divine Mercy in its presentations.

> "On January 4, 1997, exactly one year from the day the Life Foundation Ministries obtained the negative of the Vilnius image, the first samples of the enlarged image came off the press and representatives of Life Foundation Ministries brought one out to be viewed by the benefactors. As the image was unrolled, the light from a nearby corridor illuminated the print from behind, producing as though a translucent presence of the Lord in the midst of those gathered there. The sight made a profound impression upon all the observers.

> The Founder of the presentation noted, however, that, although in the words of the Divine Mercy Chaplet we pray: 'For the sake of his sorrowful Passion, have mercy on us and on the whole world,' there isn't much evidence in The Divine Mercy Image of Our Lord's sufferings; it is a portrayal of His risen, glorified body.' To that another

---

201 Fr. Seraphim Michalenko, MIC, "The Holy Shroud and the Image of The Divine Mercy According to blessed Faustina Kowalska," *The Holy Face Symposium* (Rome, Italy, October 1999) pp. 248-249.

member of the Foundation [202] replied, that there exists an image that does reveal the Lord's great sufferings - the Holy Shroud of Turin. At this point another member of the Foundation recalled that someone had sent them prints of the bust of the Holy Shroud and promptly brought one out, intending to place the images side-by-side for the purpose of making a comparison. She was moved, instead, to superimpose the image of the Shroud over the Divine Mercy Image. As she did that, the light from the corridor caused the Divine Mercy Image to shine through the Shroud Image, revealing a breath-taking coincidence of the faces." [203]

Overwhelmed by what they had witnessed, Life Foundation Ministries contacted The Shroud of Turin Research Project in Colorado Springs. They wanted to know what was wrong with their findings.

After several hours of tests they were told that it seemed there was nothing wrong with their conclusions. Not only did the faces match in multiple points of convergence and appear to be identical, but also the length of the hands and the width of the shoulders were the same.

Although this was not a scientific process, it appears that the Shroud of Turin and Vilnius Image of Divine Mercy are identical. To test their findings to make sure it was not a fluke, they tried the convergence with other renditions of the Image other than the Vilnius Image. NONE OF THEM MATCH- and, in fact, all the others are grossly distorted.

Although the Catholic Church has not ruled on the authenticity of the Shroud of Turin, it appears that only the Vilnius Image of Divine Mercy matches the pattern that Sr. Faustina saw and directed the artist, Mr. Kazimierowski, to paint. [204]

And now we may know one reason why Jesus said *"It isn't good, but it's good enough..."* It is *good enough* to show that the Original Image of Divine Mercy of Vilnius, and only the Vilnius Image of Divine Mercy, follows the pattern that Jesus wanted painted: a portrait of Jesus whose pattern is verified by the Shroud of Turin.

Why would anyone want any Image of Divine Mercy other than the Vilnius Image of Divine Mercy, *a portrait commissioned by Jesus Christ Himself?*

---

202 Elizabeth Hackett, present president of *Life Foundation* Ministries, a personal friend and co-worker with the author.

203 Michalenko, *op.cit.,* p. 249

204 This phenomenon can be viewed in the Life Foundation Ministries' DVD "A Message of Hope and Healing," which has been shown for many years on EWTN (Eternal Word Television Network), the Global Catholic Network.

Obviously, this is how Jesus desires to picture himself to us as the Divine Mercy. As Fr. Andrasz, S.J., said:

> "The vision of the Merciful Jesus in this particular representation occurred repeatedly during sister Faustina's lifetime. Our Savior evidently wanted the image to be deeply impressed upon her soul." [205]

For whatever purpose would Jesus continually present Himself in this manner other than He wanted Himself to painted as in that vision. Seems like a commissioning to me. So it seemed to St. Faustina since she kept wanting the painting to be corrected and corrected to come close to how Jesus presented Himself to her in the vision.

It is the portrait of Jesus which St. Faustina identifies as the *Throne of His Mercy*. It is the Image whose power and graces the Devil wanted destroyed with the Diary of St. Faustina. It is *The only portrait that Jesus ever Commissioned.* [206]

For all these reasons that I have presented in this manuscript I only venerate the original Vilnius Image of Divine Mercy and recommend it to others.

NOTE: Please read the important Addendum that follows.

---

205 Andrasz, S.J., *op.cit.*, p. 24.
206 Copyright by the author 2004

Addendum to Chapter 5
The Image of Divine Mercy

After my manuscript was rejected by several major Catholic publishing houses, I decided to submit a copy to an acquaintance closely associated with the Mission of Divine Mercy, hoping for an endorsement and/or help in getting it published.

After four months (!) I received my copy back with detailed notations. However, one set of comments upset me to my core, since it accused me of making inaccurate statements and drawing false conclusions. I sent an email back to the acquaintance and said:

> "I am in the process of reviewing them all (comments). When finished I will make an appointment with my censor and headship (he is my pastor). I will follow his suggestions, guidance and direction."

When I talked to my censor, much to my surprise he told me that he had also been sent a copy of the comments. Surprised? Yes, since my accuser never had the courtesy to tell me what my accuser had done. It appeared that I was being outflanked to make sure that the censor had the comments and accusations. To me this action implied I might not have the integrity to contact the censor myself.

My censor agrees that the accusations and conclusions of my accuser are erroneous and so he says the manuscript stands as governed by the original *Nihil Obstat* and there are no additional matters of Faith or Morals to be visited.

Because my accuser's action has future implications of further *public* actions against my conclusions, I will address these accusations in this addendum so as to preclude an expansion of the accusations into another forum after this book is published. To appraise the reader of what has happened, I will quote the statements of my accuser without divulging the accuser's identity.

> "…here you bring your personal observations to conclusions that are not true and make a freethinking statement – Jesus did *not* commission the Vilnus Image, Jesus instructed St. Faustina to 'pain (*sic*) an image according to the pattern you see…" (Diary 47) – she tried but found her efforts lacking – thus Blessed Michael Sopocko took up the task with Mother Irene's permission and engaged the artist Kazimirowski to paint the image. Thus the words in Diary 47-48 were fulfilled: "**Paint an image according to the pattern you see, with the signature: Jesus, I trust in You. I desire that this image be venerated, first in your chapel, and (then) throughout the world. I promise that the soul that will venerate this image will not perish. I also promise victory over (its) enemies already here on earth, especially at the hour of death. I Myself will defend it as My own glory.**" In Diary 313 you must note St. Faustina' reactions to the paining (*sic*) and Jesus' words to her – 'I said to the Lord, 'Who will paint You as beautiful as You are?' Then I heard these words: **Not in the beauty of the color, nor of the brush lies the greatness of this image, but in My grace.**" Thus you should not and cannot make the preferential statement without a qualification that Jesus Himself makes – if you express your preference you must qualify that the Vilnus Image is NOT the only one to which the grace of Jesus is given. I trust you understand the seriousness of what you have do on this point and trust you will clarify what is the truth. The theological truth of the ICON is what is basic – *it is the Pattern as presented by Jesus of Himself that must be in the Divine Mercy Image* – additions of heart, crown, etc. do not meet the elements of "the Pattern" and should be avoided and discouraged."

Although the accuser's conclusion is not presented in the format of a formal logic argument it fits the pattern of a *"non-sequitur"* (Latin for '*it does not follow*') argument in which the conclusion DOES NOT FOLLOW FROM THE PREMISE. If presented in that format it might read:

> "The Vilnus Image is the only portrait that Jesus commissioned, therefore it is the only image "to which the grace of Jesus is given."

I categorically deny that I believe or imply that conclusion.

First, the accuser attacks the statement that St. Faustina was commissioned because it was Blessed Michael Sopocko who got the artist and set up the painting sessions. I wonder what part of Chapter 5 the accuser did not read. I have very explicitly stated that many times. If the objection is to word "commissioned" because St. Faustina did not actually paint or get the artist, therefore she was not "commissioned," then I suggest a revisiting the dictionary's definition of commission: *"The act of committing or giving authority to carry out a particular task or duty, or granting certain powers, an entrusting."* I think her authority is well stated in the Diary and in this chapter.

One of her confessors, Fr. Joseph Andrasz, S.J., says:

> "The vision of the Merciful Jesus in this particular representation occurred repeatedly during Sister Faustina's lifetime. Our Savior evidently *wanted the image to be deeply impressed upon her soul.*" [207]

Since St. Faustina was the only person given this pattern (*"...having it deeply impressed upon her soul"*) Blessed Michael Sopocko had to get Mother Irene's permission to have St. Faustina present at times to judge the accuracy of the painting since she is the only who has seen Jesus as He presents Himself in the Pattern He desired to be followed. Blessed Michael Sopocko obviously knew that it was St. Faustina and only St. Faustina that could express what the pattern was since he states he wondered what this image would look like, having no idea himself. And obviously, St. Faustina understood that Jesus was presenting Himself with all His beauty and she desired to make the image look just like Him; "Who will paint You as beautiful as You are?" (Sounds like a portrait to me).

As to the standards of icons, I believe I did a magnificent job of presenting them by quoting from *The Spirit of the Liturgy* by Joseph Cardinal Ratzinger, now Pope Benedict XVI. I don't think I missed any important points about icons!

However, the accuser states: *"The theological truth of the ICON is what is basic-it is the Pattern as presented by Jesus of Himself that must be in the Divine Mercy Image..."* Chapter 5 is replete with my arguments that following the pattern was important and paramount. Yet I have never heard any criticism of the Hyla still hanging in the Convent where lay the remains of St. Faustina – the Image that so upset Fr. Sopocko who enumerated its faults, especially the fact it did not follow the "pattern," and whose comments I have quoted in this chapter. If as my accuser states: "The theological truth of the ICON is what is basic-it is the Pattern as presented by Jesus of Himself that must be in the Divine Mercy Image..." then why is the Hyla still sold in the gift shops? I hope they are not following the example of Mr. Adolf Hyla who answered

---

207 Joseph Andrasz, S.J., *Divine Mercy... We Trust in You!* (Stockbridge, MA: Marian Helpers, 1986), p. 24.

Blessed Michael Sopocko that "…he is going to paint the kind of image that those commissioning him are going to want" even though Blessed Michael Sopocko states:

> "The Hyla image must have been painted in 1946, since I already found it in 1947 and I ascertained the following deficiencies: blatant feminism – the whole figure is curved (as though dancing); the right hand raised too high, expressing action (drama or comedy), and not composure (serenity); the rays overly materialistic, like ropes; a skittish look directed somewhere into space; an inappropriate background (formerly there were flowers, and now a tile floor and the blue of the sky – no logic)… [208]

> When I came (to Cracow) from Wilno (August 1947), I brought to the attention of the Sisters of Our Lady of Mercy that that image does not correspond at all to Sr. Faustina's vision, and I asked Mr. Hyla to correct it and not to paint such images anymore. Unfortunately, Mr. Hyla did not come into line with my observations (remarks) and said point-blank that he is going to paint the kind of images that those commissioning him are going to want, and he executed a couple hundred of them against a variety of backgrounds… [209]

> …Mr. Hyla's stubbornness *and that of the people who distribute his images is negatively disposing the Bishops, the cause of devotion to The Divine Mercy, and to me, because – as I recently found out – they impute to me that I not only tolerate this, but even support it, up to now, in order to avoid conflict, I kept silent, but from now on, for the good of the cause, I have to tell the truth.* [210]

If Fr. Sopocko had all this to say as to how the Hyla does not follow the pattern Jesus wanted reproduced, then my conclusion is that the Hyla cannot meet the standards to be "The Throne of Mercy" St. Faustina states *"O sweet Jesus, it is here You established the throne of Your mercy…"* in Diary Entry 1and Footnote 2 identifies as "The Image."

Now as to the accusation that I state that the Vilnus Image is the only image to which Jesus gives His grace. Nothing could be farther from the truth of my belief in the Doctrine of Grace. And since my censor understood that there was not even the least implication in my statement that the accusation

---

208 Stackpole, *op. cit.*, p82
209 *Ibid.* p. 86
210 *Ibid.* pp. 87-8.

was correct, he concluded no further revisiting of the *Nihil Obstat* was necessary.

But to be categorically understood I write the following:

This author knows and believes that grace is *"the gratuitous gift that God makes to us of his own life"* (*Catechism* 1999), and only He can give Grace.

This author knows and believes that when a person prays before a relic of saint to ask the intercession of the saint for a miracle or some other grace, that if granted, that neither the relic nor the saint is the *source of the grace*, but only the instrument which God has chosen to use to honor the saint.

This author knows and believes that God has the freedom to use a non believer to effect Grace for His people as attested to by the Lord's use of Cyrus, King of Persia, whom He calls *"His anointed one"* (Isaiah 45:1) and directs him even though Cyrus does not know Him (Isaiah 45: 5). Cyrus issues the decree for the captives to return from Babylon to rebuild the Temple of God in Jerusalem (Ezra 6: 1-5).

This author knows and believes that God can use an antagonist or enemy and turn his actions from a curse to a blessing as attested to the story of Balaam, the pagan prophet, sent by King Balak to curse Israel his enemy sojourning in the wilderness. Balaam saw that Yahweh was pleased to bless Israel and Balaam gives one of the most important prophecies concerning the Messiah: *"I see him –but not in the present. I perceive him-but not close at hand: a star is emerging from Jacob, a scepter is rising from Israel...* (Numbers 24: 17).

This author knows and believes that God does not have to use any instrument, but can act directly as witnessed by terminally ill patients seeing a vision or hearing a voice that indicates they will be healed and then are instantaneously healed.

Since Blessed Michael Sopocko told Hyla not to paint anymore Divine Mercy Images could one draw the conclusion that Blessed Sopocko thought that the graces of Jesus couldn't flow through them?

Of course not!

The obvious reason he wanted Hyla to stop was because he wasn't following the pattern that Jesus had shown to St. Faustina. The Pattern is important as

I have thoroughly explained and to which my accuser agrees as attested to by my accuser's own quote:

> "The theological truth of the ICON is what is basic – it is the Pattern as presented by Jesus of Himself that must be in the Divine Mercy Image – additions of heart, crown, etc. do not meet the elements of "the Pattern" and should be avoided and discouraged."

Sounds like my accuser is using a double standard against me!

As for my statement that *"The Vilnus Image of Divine Mercy is the only portrait Jesus ever commissioned."* I am emphasizing that it is the only image that is attested to by *Jesus* to meet at least His minimum standards of the pattern, since He says to St. Faustina: **'It is not good, but it is good enough."** That is the complete and total reason for my statement. Until someone can categorically prove that another image follows the pattern which Blessed Fr. Michael Sopocko understood that only St. Faustina knew and could pass judgment on, since she is the only one "given authority to carry out this action" (commissioned) to have a image painted even though she could not paint, or another Image of Divine Mercy that was declared "Good enough" by Jesus, I stand by my statement.

Anytime the words "this Image" or "the Image" is read or found in the Diary of St. Faustina, it refers to the Vilnius Image of Divine Mercy, the only one in existence during the life time of St. Faustina.

The reader is free to accept or reject my conclusions and the statement that "The Original Vilnus Image of Divine Mercy is the only portrait Jesus ever commissioned."

It is *not* a matter of Faith and Morals!

But why would you want any other Image?

If the Original Vilnius Image of Divine Mercy is "good enough" for Jesus, it sure is good enough for this author.

Chapter 6
The Novena and the Feast of Divine Mercy

Introduction to Chapter 6
The Novena and the Feast of Divine Mercy

Although practiced by many, the Novena of Divine Mercy in conjunction with the Feast of Divine Mercy is one of the least understood devotions of Divine Mercy.

As I traveled the United States teaching and preaching on Divine Mercy many questions were asked about the Novena and many thoughts proffered that were just not true.

So in 2007 in preparation for Divine Mercy Sunday I scheduled several talks to education the people of my parish, St. Thomas Aquinas, Rio Rancho, NM. Many from the Albuquerque area also attended. I gave my talks and during the Question and Answer period most of the questions were on the Novena: What exactly is it? What are the requirements to practice it correctly? What were the benefits?

So when 2008 came round I did further research into it and found much new material. I used the book *Pillars of Fire in My Soul,* edited by Dr. Robert Stackpole, which contained for the first time a translation of *"The Essential Features of the Devotion to the Divine Mercy,"* by Reverend Ignacy Rozycki, S.T.D., given at a symposium in Cracow celebrating the 50the anniversary of the revelation given to St. Faustina. This paper is really a summary of the essentials of Father Rozycki's main work, a massive tome, he prepared at the request of John Paul II, then the Cardinal of Cracow. (I look forward to the publication of the complete work by the John Paul II Institute of Divine Mercy which is having it translated at the present time.)

As I prepared my notes for the 2008 lecture series, I was also researching material for the teaching I would do on the *"Seven Feast of Yahweh"* in 2009. I began to see many correlations between the Feast of *Rosh Hashanah,* the

Days of Awe, and *Yom Kippur* and Good Friday, the 9 day novena to Divine Mercy and the Feast of Mercy.

All this material coalesced by the time I did my Divine Mercy series of teachings in the Phoenix, Arizona area over Divine Mercy Sunday, and I present the result, in this chapter.

The Novena and the Feast of Divine Mercy

The Feast of Divine Mercy, which John Paul II established in 2000, [211] is celebrated on the Second Sunday of Easter and arises out of a series of apparitions received by a Polish nun, Sr. Faustina. Sr. Faustina was born in Poland in 1905. When she was twenty years old she entered the Congregation of the Sisters of Our Lady of Mercy where she lived for the next thirteen years until her death on October 5, 1938.

In her Diary Jesus says:

> **"... I desire that the first Sunday after Easter be the Feast of Mercy.**
>
> **+Ask of my faithful servant [Father Sopocko] that, on this day, he tell the whole world of My great mercy; that whoever approaches the Fount of Life on this day will be granted complete remission of sins and punishment.**
>
> **+Mankind will not have+ peace until it turns with trust to My mercy...**
>
> **My Heart rejoices in this title of Mercy."** [212]

She was beatified by Pope John Paul II in 1993 and canonized in 2000. When canonizing her, the Pope said,

> "Today my joy is truly great in presenting the life and witness of Sr.

---

211   See Appendix B
212   Diary, Entries 299-300.

Faustina to the whole Church as a gift of God for our time. By Divine Providence, the life of this humble daughter of Poland was completely linked with the history of the 20th century, the century we have just left behind. In fact, it was between the First and Second World Wars that Christ entrusted his message of mercy to her. Those who remember, who were witnesses and participants in the events of those years and the horrible sufferings they caused for millions of people know well how necessary was this message of mercy." [213]

In April 1978, the Holy See permitted spread of this devotion. This does not mean that you are required to believe in the apparitions or practice this devotion since it is a private revelation. The Catechism of the Catholic Church says this about private revelations:

"67 Throughout the ages, there have been so-called "private" revelations, some of which have been recognized by the authority of the Church. They do not belong, however, to the deposit of faith. It is not their role to improve or complete Christ's definitive Revelation, but to help live more fully by it in a certain period of history. Guided by the magisterium of the Church, the *sensus fidelium* [214] knows how to discern and welcome in these revelations whatever constitutes an authentic call of Christ or his saints to the Church.

Christian faith cannot accept "revelations" that claim to surpass or correct the Revelation of which Christ is the fulfillment, as is the case in certain non-Christian religions and also in certain recent sects which base themselves on such "revelations." [215]

However, you are free to do so and free to spread the devotion since the Church has found nothing in it contrary to our faith. The one primarily responsible for the Holy See approving the authenticity of the apparitions was Karol Cardinal Wojtyla, then Archbishop of Krakow. Later he was elected Pope and took the name John Paul II. In 1981 he said his destined role was to bring the era of Divine Mercy into the world.

---

213   *L'Osservatore Romano*, Weekly Edition in English, 3 May 2000, page 1
214   "A supernatural appreciation of the faith shown by the universal consent in matters of faith and morals manifested by the whole body of the faithful under the guidance of the Magisterium." Cf. *Catechism of the Catholic Church*, p. 899.
215   *Catechism of the Catholic Church*, #67.

"Right from the beginning of my ministry in St Peter's See in Rome I consider this message my special task. Providence has assigned it to me in the present situation of man, the Church and the world. It could be said that precisely this situation assigned that message to me as my task before God" [216]

Saint Faustina was born Helena Kowalska in the village of Glogowiec west of Lodz, Poland, on August 25, 1905. She was the third of ten children. When she was almost twenty, she entered the Congregation of the Sisters of Our Lady of Mercy, whose members devote themselves to the care and education of troubled young women.

The following year she received her religious habit and was given the name Sister Maria Faustina, to which she added *"of the Most Blessed Sacrament,"* as was permitted by her Congregation. [217]

In the 1930's, Sister Faustina received from the Lord a message of mercy that she was told to spread throughout the world. She was asked to become the *apostle* and *secretary* of God's mercy, a model of how to be merciful to others, and an instrument for reemphasizing God's plan of mercy for the world.

It was not a glamorous prospect. Her entire life, in imitation of Christ, was to be a sacrifice [218] – a life lived for others. At the Divine Lord's request, she willingly offered her personal sufferings in union with Him to atone for the sins of others. In her daily life she was to become a doer of mercy, bringing joy and peace to others, and by writing about God's mercy she was to encourage others to trust in Him and thus prepare the world for His coming again. [219]

Convinced of her own unworthiness and terrified at the thought of trying to write anything, she nonetheless began keeping a diary in 1934 in obedience to the express wishes of her spiritual director, Fr. Michael Sopocko. [220] For four years she recorded divine revelations and mystical experiences, together with her own inmost thoughts, insights, and prayers. Eventually, Jesus Himself directed her to continue the writings in her diary giving her personal dictation and calling her His *"Secretary of Divine Mercy."* [221]

The result is a book of some 600 printed pages that, in simple language, repeats and clarifies the gospel story of God's love for His people, emphasizing,

---

216 November 22, 1981 at the Shrine of Merciful Love in Collevalenza, Italy
217 Diary, FN 105
218 *Ibid.*, Entry 135
219 *Ibid.*, Entry 429
220 *Ibid.*, FN 42
221 *Ibid.*, Entry 965.

above all, the need to trust in His loving, merciful action in all the aspects of our lives.

She wrote and suffered in secret, with only her spiritual director and some of her superiors aware that anything special was taking place in her life. After her death from tuberculosis in 1938, even her closest associates were amazed as they began to discover what great sufferings and deep mystical experiences had been given to this sister of theirs, who had always been so cheerful and humble. She had taken deeply into her heart God's gospel command to *"Be merciful even as your heavenly Father is merciful"* [222] as well as her confessor's directive that she should act in such a way that everyone who came in contact with her would go away joyful.

One of the outgrowths of the devotion is the Novena of Divine Mercy. What is a novena?

> "Novena is a cycle of prayers spanning nine days, usually one day a week for nine consecutive weeks. It consists of prescribed prayers and devotions and usually includes the reception of the Sacraments of Penance and Holy Eucharist. A novena may be made in common in church or in private. The *Raccolta* lists 36 novenas that are indulgenced by the Church. The practice is commemorative of the 'Novena of the Apostles,' that is, the days spent in prayer by them in the Cenacle between the Ascension and Pentecost (Acts 1: 13-14), and the only novena that should be observed in parochial churches is that preceding the feast of Pentecost." [223]

When you go into the Diary to find references to the Novena of Divine Mercy you will only find one *serial* entry (1209-1230) that deals specifically with the Novena. And it does not include the Chaplet. However, a novena of Chaplets before the Feast of Divine Mercy is mentioned several times (714, 851, and 1059).

When you read the Diary did you become confused and wonder why the entries do not seem to follow one another like a normal diary?

There is a reason for this. But you won't find it in the diary itself. Sister Faustina alludes to this when she writes: *"I make no mention here* [224] *of the various visions and graces God granted me during this time, because I've written this down elsewhere."* And if you go looking to find them in the diary you will miss the footnote at the end of the sentence.

---

222 Luke 6: 36
223 Broderick, Robert C., editor, *The Catholic Encyclopedia* (Nashville, KY: Thomas Nelson Publisher) 1986, p. 425.
224 Diary, Entry 130

Once you go to that footnote 42 we read:

"This is elsewhere in the diary. For a long time Sister Faustina did not take notes of her experiences and of graces received. It was only at the explicit order of her confessor, Father Sopocko, that she began to write down her experiences as they occurred, and also earlier ones as she remembered them. After some time, she burned her notes. Father Sopocko gives the following account; 'When I was in the Holy Land for a few weeks, she was persuaded by a supposed angel to burn the diary. As penance, I told her to reconstruct the part destroyed. But in the meantime new experience came, and she wrote down new and old things alternately. Hence the lack of chronological order in the diary."[225]

Fr. Sopocko gives more details in another account:

"In 1934 I went to Palestine and was not in Vilnius for some months… When I came back, Sister Faustina told me that she had burned the diary she had written so far. She said that on a certain occasion a young man appeared to her and said that the writing was no use and could only be a source of anxieties and he ordered her to throw the diary into the fire, which she did. I told her that she had not done well, that this had been a temptation from the devil, and I requested her to try to re-create what she could remember from that diary, and continue to write a diary." [226]

There are many things that are not explained in the diary and many details are missing. We would probably never know how the Novena came together with the Chaplet if Fr. Sopocko hadn't kept detailed notes of his own. Now that he himself is called Blessed and is up for canonization we are able to scrutinize all of his writings. We find great insights into Sr. Faustina's experiences.

How did this devotion begin then?

Sr. Faustina was directed to say the Novena.[227] And the fact that she was commanded by Jesus to write everything down to spread the Cult of Divine Mercy the Novena was naturally seen as a direction to devotees also. Therefore, Fr. Sopocko began to publish the devotion.

---

225 *Ibid.*, FN 42
226 Maria Tarnawska, *Sister Faustina Kowalska—Her Life and Mission* (Stockbridge, MA: Marian Helpers) 1989 p. 160-1.
227 Diary, Entry 796.

Since Sr. Faustina left Vilnius on March 21, 1936 and the Public Veneration of the Image of Divine Mercy and the Feast of Divine Mercy were all left in the hands of Fr. Sopocko. In 1936 he published a pamphlet titled "Divine Mercy." And one year later a second booklet call "Divine Mercy in the Liturgy."

> "...The subject became widely known only when, at the end of August 1937, Father Sopocko, visiting Cracow, had the opportunity to talk for some time with Sister Faustina and to look at her diary written after she had left Vilnius. Their meeting was fruitful, as Father Sopocko himself informs us: 'I found in her diary a novena to the Divine Mercy which I very much liked. When I asked her where she had it from, she told me that Jesus Himself had dictated to her this novena. Prior to this, Jesus had taught her a chaplet to the Divine Mercy, and other prayers, which I decided to publish.'" [228]

Fr. Sopocko published these verbatim with a series of invocations in the diary that he collected into a litany in a small booklet titled: "*Chrystus Krol Milosierdzia*" or "Christ the King of Mercy." [229] He did this with the help of the Superior, Mother Irene. Two months later, Sr. Faustina saw the booklet and wrote in diary:

> "...Then I entered into an intimate conversation with the Lord, thanking Him for having condescended to grant me the grace of seeing how the veneration of His unfathomable mercy is spreading..." [230]

Then she writes later:

> "...As I was glancing through it, Jesus gave me to know interiorly: **'Already there are many souls who have been drawn to My love by this image. My mercy acts in souls through this work...**" [231]

The devotion spread very rapidly and then was banned in 1959 [232] because of a faulty translation caused by the fact the Sr. Faustian only had a 3rd grade education and wrote phonetically. This was prophesized in the Diary:

---

228 Tarnawska, *op.cit.*, pp. 298-9.
229 Dairy, FN 208
230 *Ibid.*, Entry 1300
231 *Ibid.*, Entry 1379
232 Robert Stackpole, STD, editor, *Pillars of Fire in My Soul* (Stockbridge, MA: Marian Press) 2003, pp. 15-6.

"Once as I was talking with my spiritual director, I had an interior vision — quicker than lightning — of his soul in great suffering, in such agony that God touches very few souls with such fire. The suffering arises from this work. There will come a time when this work, which God is demanding so very much, will be as though utterly undone. And then God will act with great power, which will give evidence of its authenticity. It will be a new splendor for the Church, although it has been dormant in it from long ago..." [233]

Coupled with the writing and intermingling of concurrent and recalled entries, much confusion resulted. The Cardinal Archbishop of Krakow, Karl Wojtyla, in 1965, asked Father Ignacy Rozycki, Doctor of Dogmatic theology to study the Diary in manuscript form, to make a *"critical analysis of the Diary and letters of Sister Faustina as part of the Informative Process concerning life and virtues."* [234]

He had heard rumors about these writings and did not want to waste his time on the hallucinations of an uneducated nun. But before writing a letter of refusal he decided to skim through the work, *"just to pass the time."* After several pages he changed his mind.

A retranslated diary was submitted it to Rome for reinstatement. The ban was lifted in 1979 when the Vatican wrote

"...there no longer exists, on the part of this Sacred Congregation, any impediment to the spreading of the devotion to The Divine Mercy in the authentic forms proposed by the Religious Sister [i.e., the Servant of God, Faustina Kowalska]." [235]

Fr. Rozycki devoted several years to writing a massive tome of 500 pages in French promoting the devotion theologically. [236]

"On February 19-20, 1981, at a symposium in Krakow celebrating the 50th anniversary of the revelations given to Sr. Faustina, he presented a lecture entitled "The Essential Features of the devotion to The Divine Mercy." [237]

---

233 Diary, Entry 378
234 Stackpole, *op.cit.,* p.91
235 *Ibid.,* p. 17.
236 *Ibid.,* p. 92.
237 *Ibid.,* pp. 91-2

Some parts have been published by The John Paul II Institute of Divine Mercy, in the book, *Pillars of Fire in My Soul.*

The main focus is on the Feast of Divine Mercy and the extraordinary graces attached to its celebration. He found that the Mass formulary for the second Sunday of Easter *"with only slight changes"* could *"serve as a Mass dedicated to Divine Mercy."* [238]

Jesus commands Sister Faustina to prepare for the Feast of The Divine Mercy with a novena. [239] Later Jesus tells her:

"...On each day you will bring to My Heart a different group of souls, and you will immerse them in this ocean of My Mercy, and I will bring all these souls into the house of My Father. You will do this in this life and in the next..." [240]

To which Sister Faustina responds:

"'...Jesus, I do not know how to make this novena or which souls to bring first into Your Most Compassionate Heart.' Jesus replied that He would tell me which souls to bring each day into His Heart." [241]

Sister Faustina in another entry says:

"The Lord told me to say this chaplet for nine days before the Feast of Mercy. It is to begin on Good Friday. **By this novena, I will grant every possible grace to souls.**" [242]

Referring to this entry, Fr. Rozycki states:

"The words 'all possible graces' mean that the person saying the novena to the Divine Mercy will obtain all the benefits of God he asks for, *regardless of whether he requests these graces for himself or for others.*" [243]

There are many demands Jesus makes concerning the Feast: what is its

---

238 *Ibid.*, p. 112.
239 Diary, Entry 1059
240 *Ibid.*, Entry 1209
241 *Ibid.*
242 Diary, entry 796
243 Stackpole, *op.cit.*, p. 112.

purpose, how it is to be celebrated solemnly, but most importantly that it is to be a liturgical feast of the universal Church:

1. The Image of Divine Mercy that Jesus commissioned is to be an intimate part of the celebration of the Feast of Divine Mercy, being publicly blessed and venerated on that day:

"…And Jesus said to me, **And who knows anything about this feast? No one! Even those who should be proclaiming My mercy and teaching people about it often do not know about it themselves. That is why I want the image to be solemnly blessed on the first Sunday after Easter, and I want it to be venerated publicly so that every soul may know about it…"** [244]

"…**I am making you the administrator of My mercy. Tell the confessor that the Image is to be on view in the church and not within the enclosure in that convent. By means of this Image I shall be granting many graces to souls; so let every soul have access to it."** [245]

"…**I desire that this image be venerated, first in your chapel,** *and [then] throughout the world… I promise that the soul that will venerate this image will not perish.* **I also promise victory over [its] enemies already here on earth, especially at the hour of death. I Myself will defend it as My own glory** [246]

2. A Novena to the Divine Mercy in conjunction with the Chaplet of Divine Mercy is to be associated with the Feast:

"Novena to The Divine Mercy[206] which Jesus instructed me to write down and make before the Feast of Mercy. It begins on Good Friday. **I desire that during these nine days you bring souls to the fountain of My mercy, that they may draw there from strength and refreshment and whatever grace they need in the hardships of life, and especially at the hour of death…"** [247]

"The Lord told me to say this chaplet for nine days before the Feast

---

244 Diary Entry 341.
245 *Ibid.*, Entry 570
246 *Ibid.*, Entries 47-8
247 *Ibid.*, Entry 1209.

of Mercy. It is to begin on Good Friday. **By this novena, I will grant every possible grace to souls**" [248].

3. Priests are asked and encouraged give sermons on Jesus' *"Unfathomable Mercy"* and the most exceptional grace Jesus gives to this Feast day:

"...No soul will be justified until it turns with confidence to My mercy, and this is why the first Sunday after Easter is to be the Feast of Mercy. On that day, priests are to tell everyone about My great and unfathomable mercy..." [249]

"Ask of my faithful servant [Father Sopocko] that, on this day, he tell the whole world of My great mercy; that whoever approaches the Fount of Life Fount his day will be granted complete remission of sins and punishment..." [250]

Jesus' desire that the soul go to confession and receive communion on the Feast is more explicitly and clearly stated in the Diary:

"...I desire that the Feast of Mercy[129] **be a refuge and shelter for all souls, and especially for poor sinners. On that day the very depths of My tender mercy are open. I pour out a whole ocean of graces upon those souls who approach the fount of My mercy. The soul that will go to Confession and receive Holy Communion shall obtain complete forgiveness of sins and punishment. On that day all the divine floodgates through which grace flow are opened..."** [251]

What Fr. Rozycki goes on to say about the grace promised by Jesus is mind boggling. The most exceptional grace promised by Jesus for the Feast of the Divine Mercy is greater than a plenary indulgence which only consists of *"a remission before God of temporal punishment due to sins already forgiven,"* [252] and never the remission of sins itself. [253]

---

248 *Ibid.*, Entry 796
249 *Ibid.*, Entry 570
250 *Ibid.*, Entry 300
251 *Ibid.*, Entry 699
252 *Catechism of the Catholic Church* 1471
253 An APOSTOLIC PENITENTIARY DECREE has been granted for a Plenary Indulgence on the Feast of Divine Mercy. (See Appendix A at the end of the book.)

Fr. Rozycki continues:

"The nature of this highest grace leaves no room for any ambiguity: It is the complete remission of sins and punishment; in other words: it is the complete forgiveness of all sins, which were not yet forgiven and of all punishment due for those sins. As regards the forgiveness of sins then, this grace is equal to the grace of Baptism. In other words, Jesus raised the reception of Holy Communion on the Feast of The Divine Mercy to the rank of a "second Baptism." [254]

Theologically, there is no possibility of a second baptism. Baptism can only be received once and leaves an indelible mark on the soul. What is meant in the quote above is that its power is *like* a second baptism. The Catechism of the Church considered the Sacrament of Reconciliation as the *"second plank of salvation,"* since it restores the soul to the purity it received at Baptism. [255]

Therefore, Fr. Rozycki states:

"The grace of the complete remission of sins and punishment is theologically possible since neither this grace, nor the conditions for obtaining it contradict revealed teachings. If God is able to bestow this grace through the sacrament of Baptism, why would He not be able to bestow it – if He so wishes – through the Eucharist, which is the greatest sacrament? [256]

It is obvious that in order to effect a complete forgiveness of sins and punishment, the Holy Communion received on the Feast of Divine Mercy must not only be partaken of worthily, one must also reverently and devotedly fulfill the basic requirements of the Divine Mercy devotion. [257]

Jesus did not limit His generosity to this one exceptional grace on the Feast of Divine Mercy. He actually states that we can be inundated or drowned in graces:

"...On that day, the very depths of My Mercy are open: I pour out a whole ocean of graces upon souls who will approach the fount of My Mercy ...On that day all the Divine floodgates through which graces flow are opened..." [258]

---

254 Stackpole, *op.cit.,* p. 114
255 *Catechism of the Catholic Church* 1446
256 Stackpole, op. cit., p. 114
257 See Appendix A at the end of this book.
258 Diary Entry 699

Fr. Rozycki concludes:

"The incomparable effectiveness of this refuge is manifested in three ways. *First* it is manifested through its universality. All people, even those who never had devotion to The Divine Mercy, even sinners who repented on the day of the Feast itself, can participate to the fullest extent in all the graces which Jesus prepared for this Feast. *Secondly,* on this day, Jesus wishes to shower people not only with saving graces, but also with temporal blessings, both to individuals and to communities of people, for He said: "Mankind will not know peace until it turns to the fount of My Mercy." *Thirdly,* all graces and benefits, even in their highest degrees, are accessible on this day to everyone, as long as they are asked for with great trust. Christ did not attach such an extraordinary abundance of graces and benefits to any other form of this Devotion." [259]

This should not surprise us since Vatican II states the Eucharist is *"the source and summit of the Christian life."* [260]

If the exceptional grace of [the Communion on Divine Mercy Sunday is the main focus of the Devotion of Divine Mercy why is there a novena leading up to it, which has no exceptional graces attached to it?

Jesus is unequivocal in His statement as to the purpose of the Novena to Divine Mercy:

"I understand Your words, Lord, and the magnitude of the mercy that ought to shine in my soul. Jesus: **I know, My daughter, that you understand it and that you do everything within your power. But write this** *for the many souls* **who are often worried because they do not have the material means with which to carry out an act of mercy. Yet** *spiritual mercy,* **which requires neither permissions nor storehouses, is much more meritorious and is within the grasp of every soul.** *If a soul does not exercise mercy somehow or other, it will not obtain My mercy on the day of judgment.* **Oh, if only souls knew how to gather eternal treasure for themselves, they would not be judged, for they would forestall My judgment with their mercy.**" [261]

The statement by Jesus ... *If a soul does not exercise mercy somehow or other,*

---

259 Stackpole, *op. cit.*, p. 115
260 *Lumen Gentium* 11
261 Diary Entry 1317

it will not obtain My mercy on the Day of Judgment... should not surprise us. Jesus states the same in the beatitude: *"Blessed are the merciful: they shall have mercy shown them,"* [262] which is the only beatitude in which your reward is what you do.

In the same quote from the Diary Jesus tells us the simple way that everyone can do acts of mercy.

> **"...But write this for the many souls who are often worried because they do not have the material means with which to carry out an act of mercy.** *Yet spiritual mercy, which requires neither permissions nor storehouses, is much more meritorious and is within the grasp of every soul..."* [263]

What are spiritual acts of mercy?

> **"My daughter, if I demand through you that people revere My mercy, you should be the first to distinguish yourself by this confidence in My mercy. I demand from you deeds of mercy, which are to arise out of love for Me. You are to show mercy to your neighbors always and everywhere. You must not shrink from this or try to excuse or absolve yourself from it.**
>
> **I am giving you three ways of exercising mercy toward your neighbor: the first — by deed, the second — by word, the third— by prayer. In these three degrees is contained the fullness of mercy, and it is an unquestionable proof of love for Me. By this means a soul glorifies and pays reverence to My mercy. Yes, the first Sunday after Easter is the Feast of Mercy, but there must also be acts of mercy, and I demand the worship of My mercy through the solemn celebration of the Feast and through the veneration of the image which is painted. By means of this image I shall grant many graces to souls. It is to be a reminder of the demands of My mercy, because even the strongest (163) faith is of no avail without works**. O my Jesus, You yourself must help me in everything, because You see how very little I am, and so I depend solely on Your goodness, O God." [264]

The third means of exercising mercy toward your neighbor according to

---

262   Matthew 5: 7
263   Diary Entry 1317
264   *Ibid.*, 742

the Lord is by prayer. That is exactly what we fulfill by the Novena of Divine Mercy in conjunction with the Chaplet of Divine Mercy.

In Chapter 4, The Chaplet of Divine Mercy, I explained how the Chaplet is an extension of our priestly duty of intercession extending the merits of the Mass 24/7.

The Mass is the supreme act of Intercession of Jesus Christ when He became our substitute sacrifice once and for all. The Sacrifice of Jesus on the Cross on Good Friday is the fulfillment of the Jewish Feast of *Yom Kippur* or the Feast of Atonement.

What happens on *Yom Kippur*, or the Feast of Atonement?

The Day of Atonement is a holy day established by God in Leviticus 16.

> "Yom Kippur (literally "a day of covering" for sin, for the Holy of Holies in the Tabernacle, for the Tabernacle itself, for the altar of Incense in the Holy Place, for the priests (including the high priest), and for the sins committed in by the people of Israel. An everlasting statute, it was the once-a-year, awe-inspiring zero hour for an impure nation, a nation that was required to stand clean, or holy, before the Lord." [265]

The High Priest officiates in the Temple only one time a year: on *Yom Kippur*. When in the temple he is vested in the most glorious robes from head to foot. [266] On the Feast of *Yom Kippur* he, and he *alone,* is to enter the Holy of Holies and sprinkle blood over the Mercy Seat. He must take off his glorious robes, bathe 5 times, then put on a plain white linen tunic with a cincture and enter the Holy of Holies barefooted. [267]

The *Catechism of the Catholic Church* states this about *Yom Kippur*:

> "The name of the Savior God was invoked only once in the year by the high priest in atonement for the sins of Israel, after he had sprinkled the mercy seat in the Holy of Holies with the sacrificial blood. The mercy seat was the place of God's presence. When St. Paul speaks of Jesus whom "God put forward as expiation by his blood," he means that in Christ's humanity "God was in Christ reconciling the world to himself." [268]

---

265 Bruce Scott, *The Feasts of Israel* (Bellmawr, NJ; The Friends of Israel Gospel Ministry, Inc.) 1997, p. 88.

266 Exodus 39: 1-26

267 Leviticus 16: 3-4

268 *Catechism* 433

The *Catechism* continues:

"Jesus, Israel's Messiah and therefore the greatest in the kingdom of heaven, was to fulfill the Law by keeping it in its all-embracing detail—according to his own words, down to the least of these commandments." He is in fact the only one who could keep it perfectly. On their own admission the Jews were never able to observe the Law in its entirety without violating the least of its precepts. This is why every year on the Day of Atonement the children of Israel ask God's forgiveness for their transgression of the Law. The Law indeed makes up one inseparable whole, and St. James recalls, "Whoever keeps the whole law but fails in one point has become guilty of all of it." [269]

That is how Jesus showed Himself to St. Faustina and is depicted in the original Vilnius Image of Divine Mercy. He is the High Priest (Hebrews 7: 15 to Hebrews 10: 18).

"Such is the high priest that met our need, holy, innocent and uncontaminated, set apart from sinners, and raised up above the heavens; [27] he has no need to offer sacrifices every day, as the high priests do, first for their own sins and only then for those of the people; this he did once and for all by offering himself. [28] The Law appoints high priests who are men subject to weakness; but the promise on oath, which came after the Law, appointed the Son who is made perfect for ever." [270]

Bruce Scott in his book, *The Feasts of Israel*, summarizes the time between *Rosh Hashanah and Yom Kippur* this way:

"The most consequential facet attributed to the Day of Atonement in rabbinical teaching, however, is that it is the day on which God's judgment of an individual is sealed. Ten days before, on Rosh Hashanah (New Year) (the seventh Calendar month, usually September – October timeframe), it is believed that God decides whether or not a person's name is inscribed in the Book of Life. *From Rosh Hashanah through Yom Kippur inclusively, called the ten days of Awe or Penitence, a person is admonished to sincerely repent. On Rosh Hashanah (New Year) the*

---

269 Ibid., 578
270 Hebrews 7: 26-28

greeting is, "May you be inscribed [in the Book of Life]", while on Yom Kippur the greeting is "May you be sealed [in the Book of Life]." [271]

The "Ten days of Awe" are actually a nine day novena for people to intercede for themselves and do acts of mercy ("righteous acts" as they call them) for their neighbors.

For the Rabbis said:

> "The ten days between Rosh Hashanah and Yom Kippur were set aside for prayer and supplication, because all earthly life is judged on Rosh Hashanah, and he who returns to God is forgiven on Yom Kippur, as it is written in the Mishnah (Rabbinical commentary on the Scriptures) (*Taanit* II.1), 'Brothers, it was not said of the men of Nineveh that 'God saw their sackcloth and fasting,' but rather that "God saw their works, that they turned from their evil way (Jonah 3: 10). From this we learn how great is Teshuvah, since it can tear up the evil decree, as it is said (Isaiah 6: 10): 'Return and be healed,' and it is said (Jeremiah 3: 14): 'Return, O backsliding children.'" [272]

The Feast of *Yom Kippur*, Atonement, as well as the whole sacrificial system of the ancient Jews speaks of a God who wants to forgive, who has mercy and is merciful.

Our Novena of Divine Mercy begins on Good Friday (when Jesus fulfills the Day of Atonement) and goes to Saturday before the Second Sunday of Easter, the Feast of Divine Mercy (9 days). During this time we intercede with Spiritual Acts of Mercy. (See *The Novena to Divine Mercy* at Appendix C.)

We act in our priestly role of intercession with Jesus Christ. In the Pre-Vatican II Good Friday Liturgy we interceded for:

1) the Church,
2) the Pope,
3) the Bishops, Priests, Deacons, (Sub-Deacons, Acolytes, Exorcists, Lectors, etc.) and Laity of the Church,
4) Catechumens,
5) those in error,
6) the heretics and schismatics,
7) for the Jewish People,

---

271 Scott, *op.cit.*, p. 88.
272 *Mahzor Vitri*, No. 337 (*Mahzor Vitri*: Jewish halakhic-liturgical book. It was composed by Simbah ben Samuel of Vitry, a pupil of Rashin, in the late 11th cent. AD. The book gives the halakhic rulings of the liturgy for the annual cycle of weekdays,)

8) for Pagans,

Instead of a onetime intercession at the Good Friday Liturgy, Jesus asks us to extend our prayers to a full day of intercession for each special category:

Day 1) All Mankind, especially sinners,

Day 2) Souls of Priest and Religious,

Day 3) Devout and Faithful Souls,

Day 4) Those do not believe in Jesus and do not yet know Him,

Day 5) Separated Brethren,

Day 6) Meek and Humble Souls and Souls of Little Children,

Day 7) Those who venerate and glorify My mercy,

Day 8) Souls in Purgatory, and

Day 9) Souls who are lukewarm.

By performing this Novena with the Chaplet of Divine Mercy we, through our Baptismal priestly ministry, are extending the merits of the Great High Priest on Good Friday, the Day of Atonement. At the same time we are fulfilling for 9 days the desires of our Great High Priest by doing spiritual acts of mercy in preparation for receiving Holy Communion on Divine Mercy Sunday. *"Blessed are the merciful, for they shall receive mercy."*

Because of the shortage of priests only those who fall into mortal (grave) sin should ask for confession on Divine Mercy Sunday. Confession should be received during Lent before Divine Mercy Sunday. In Diary Entry 1072 St. Faustina received Confession on the Saturday before Divine Mercy Sunday.

Jesus is the fulfillment of all the Old Testament to include its Feasts. He is our Passover Lamb and the Great High Priest of the Feast of Atonement (*Yom Kippur*). Therefore, the Novena from Good Friday to the Feast of Divine Mercy is in fulfillment of *the Days of Awe* or Repentance between *Rosh Hashanah* (the New Year) and *Yom Kippur,* the Day of Atonement.

Since our Jewish brothers believe that on *Rosh Hashanah*, three books are opened in heaven and he/she knows whether he/she is in *The Book of Life for the righteous, The Book of Life for the in-between*, or *The Book of Life for the wicked*.

In other words on *Tishri* 1 (*Rosh Hashanah*) God reviews the books of Judgment and on *Tishri* 10 (*Yom Kippur*) He metes out judgment for the year. Therefore, the days in between, the Days of Awe, or a last chance to repent before the finalized judgment.

The greeting for the New Year, *Tishri* 1, *Rosh Hashanah*, is not, *"Happy New Year,"* but *"May be you inscribed (in the Book of Life) for a good year!"*

And on *Tishri* 10, *Yom Kippur*, the greeting is: *"May you be sealed in the Book of Life."*

Does Scripture support these pious ideas?

In Exodus Moses pleaded with God in this words:

"And yet, if it pleased you to forgive their sin…! If not, please blot me out of the book you have written!' [33] Yahweh said to Moses, 'Those who have sinned against me are the ones I shall blot out of my book. " 273

David refers to this in the Psalms:

"… erase them from the book of life, do not enroll them among the upright." 274

We also find it is Psalm 139:

"Your eyes could see my embryo. In your book all my days were inscribed, every one that was fixed is there." 275

Daniel records them in his night vision:

"While I was watching,
thrones were set in place
and one most venerable took his seat.
His robe was white as snow,
the hair of his head as pure as wool.
His throne was a blaze of flames,
its wheels were a burning fire.
[10] A stream of fire poured out,
issuing from his presence.
A thousand thousand waited on him,
ten thousand times ten thousand
stood before him.
The court was in session
and the books lay open."276

And also in Daniel:

"'At that time Michael will arise—the great Prince, defender of your people. That will be a time of great distress, unparalleled since nations

---

273 Exodus 32: 32-33
274 Psalm 69: 28
275 Psalm 139: 16
276 Daniel 7; 9-10

first came into existence. When that time comes, your own people will be spared—all those whose names are found written in the Book." [277]

And when the 72 return rejoicing from their first mission, Jesus refers to these books:

"The seventy-two came back rejoicing. 'Lord,' they said, 'even the devils submit to us when we use your name.' [18] He said to them, 'I watched Satan fall like lightning from heaven. [19] Look, I have given you power to tread down serpents and scorpions and the whole strength of the enemy; nothing shall ever hurt you. [20] Yet do not rejoice that the spirits submit to you; rejoice instead that your names are written in heaven.'" [278]

And John writes in the Book of Revelation:

"Anyone who proves victorious will be dressed, like these, in white robes; I shall not blot that name out of the book of life, but acknowledge it in the presence of my Father and his angels." [279]

And the Angel revealing the New Jerusalem to John ends with these words:

"Nothing unclean may come into it: no one who does what is loathsome or false, but only those who are listed in the Lamb's book of life." [280]

If, on *Yom Kippur* our Jewish brothers believed that God decides whether or not a person's name is inscribed in the Book of Life, and the time between *Rosh Hashanah* and *Yom Kippur*, the days of Awe are for repentance, and we do a similar 9 days of good work from Good Friday to the Feast of Divine Mercy, might there be a similar book for the Feast of Divine Mercy?

St. Faustina writes in Diary:

"On one occasion, I saw the throne of the Lamb of God and before the throne three Saints: Stanislaus Kostka, Andrew Bobola and Prince Casimir, who were interceding for Poland. All at once I saw a large

---

277 Daniel 12: 1
278 Luke 10: 17-20
279 Revelation 3: 5
280 Revelation 21: 27

book which stands before the throne, and it was given to me to read. The book was written in blood. Still, I could not read anything but the name, Jesus. Then I heard a voice which said to me, **Your hour has not yet come.** Then the book was taken away from me, and I heard these words: **You will bear witness to My infinite mercy.** *In this book are written the names of the souls that have glorified My mercy.* I was overwhelmed with joy at the sight of such great goodness of God." [281]

What better symbolism to unite this diary entry to the Feast of Good Friday than the Lamb of God who was sacrificed for us in His Mercy. His Merciful Blood is used as ink to inscribe the names of those who glorify His Mercy.

I invite you to make this Novena the best you can for others. And I invite you to make it the most prayerful you have ever done *so that your name might be inscribed with the Blood of the Lamb of God in the Book of His Mercy.*

---

[281] Diary Entry 689

Chapter 7
The First Miracle of Divine Mercy

Introduction to Chapter 7
The First Miracle of Divine Mercy

I have a very inquisitive mind and many times it keeps me awake at night pondering strange questions. Such was the occasion after a meeting with my dear friends Dr. John Jackson and his wife, Rebecca, of the Shroud of Turin Institute, Colorado Springs, Colorado. She posed the question as to what might be the incident that caused the conversion of the centurion at the crucifixion.

I began a study of the details in scripture and tradition and wrote my first thoughts in a paper I hoped would be published during the Lenten season. As things would happen it was shoved to the back burner as other things became more pressing.

Then I received a called from Mary Sherron, Director, Divine Mercy Shrine at Holy Rosary Parish, Baltimore, Maryland. They were planning the 10th Anniversary celebration of the Healing of Father Ron Pytel, the former pastor, whose miraculous healing was the impetus for the Canonization of St. Faustina.

The celebration became *"A Seminar Celebrating the Teachings of St. Faustina and Divine Mercy,"* October 7 – 9, 2005.

I was not only to be the Master of Ceremonies, but to give two talks. That is when I remembered my paper on the First Miracle of Divine Mercy.

This chapter explains how the healing of the eyes of the soldier, named Longinus, at the Hour of Mercy, was the reason for the change of a town's name to Lanciano, which became the site of the first Eucharistic Heart Miracle. Coming full circle, the miracle to elevate St. Faustina to the Altar was also a heart miracle.

The First Miracle of Divine Mercy

I thought it might be of immense interest for us to find out what was the *first miracle of Divine Mercy* as the result of *"Font of Mercy"* being opened up for mankind.

In the Diary of St. Faustina, Jesus often refers to His Mercy as an *"Ocean of Mercy"*. For example, throughout the Novena of Divine Mercy (Entries 1209 -1230). He also refers to it as *"an Abyss of Mercy,"* and *"a font of Mercy."*

That moment is alluded to by Jesus Himself in the Diary:

186 +Today Jesus said to me, **I desire that you know more profoundly the love that burns in My Heart for souls, and you will understand this when you meditate upon My Passion. Call upon My mercy on behalf of sinners; I desire their (93) salvation. When you say this prayer, with a contrite heart and with faith on behalf of some sinner, I will give him the grace of conversion. This is the prayer:**

187 **"O Blood and Water, which gushed forth from the Heart of Jesus as a fount of Mercy for us, I trust in You."** [282]

However, to explain our quest to establish what the first miracle of Divine Mercy is, there are some whom we will talk to about this who will argue that the Diary of St. Faustina is only *private revelation*. [283]

---

282 Diary entries 186 and 187
283 *Catechism* 67. Throughout the ages, there have been so-called "private" revelations, some of which have been recognized by the authority of the Church. They do not belong, however, to the deposit of faith. It is not their role to improve or complete Christ's definitive Revelation, but to help live

Even though we believe it is much more than just private revelation, when supporting our arguments and facts, our two decisive weapons will be scripture and tradition. Let us start with scripture.

To establish what is the first Miracle of Divine Mercy one must know the moment at which Divine Mercy is freely available to Mankind through the Salvific Act of Jesus Christ. That moment is established by the first Pope, St. Peter, who writes in his first encyclical:

> "For you know that the price of your ransom from the futile way of life handed down from your ancestors was paid, not in anything perishable like silver or gold, [19] but in precious blood as of a blameless and spotless lamb, Christ." [284]

St. Peter states this happened for him in this way:

> "[1] Peter, apostle of Jesus Christ, to all those living as aliens in the Dispersion of Pontus, Galatia, Cappadocia, Asia and Bithynia, who have been chosen, [2] in the foresight of God the Father, to be made holy by the Spirit, obedient to Jesus Christ and *sprinkled with his blood*: Grace and peace be yours in abundance." [285]

When was Peter "*sprinkled with His Blood*?" Peter was not even present at the Crucifixion.

But all Christians are sprinkled with the Blood of Jesus when they receive the Sacraments of Initiation: Baptism, Confirmation and Eucharist.

The *Catechism of the Catholic Church* explains this in article 1225:

> In His Passover Christ opened to all men the fountain of Baptism. He had already spoken of His Passion, which he was about to suffer in Jerusalem, as a "Baptism" with which he had to be baptized (Luke 12: 50). The blood and water that flowed from the pierced side of the crucified Jesus are types of Baptism and the Eucharist, the sacraments

---

more fully by it in a certain period of history. Guided by the magisterium of the Church, the *sensus fidelium* knows how to discern and welcome in these revelations whatever constitutes an authentic call of Christ or his saints to the Church. Christian faith cannot accept "revelations" that claim to surpass or correct the Revelation of which Christ is the fulfillment, as is the case in certain non-Christian religions and also in certain recent sects which base themselves on such "revelations."

284 1 Peter 1: 18-19
285 1 Peter 1: 1-2

of new Life (cf. John 19: 34). From then on, it is possible "to be born of water and the Spirit" (John 3: 5) in order to enter the Kingdom of God..."[286]

The *Catechism* is our official link to the *"...pierced side of the crucified Jesus and the types of Baptism and the Eucharist..."* The Catechism tells us that this information comes from John. John was the only Apostle at the crucifixion, and he refers to himself as an *eyewitness*:

> "... one of the soldiers pierced his side with a lance; and immediately there came out blood and water." This is the evidence of one who saw it—true evidence, and he knows that what he says is true—and he gives it so that you may believe as well." [287]

The moment of Jesus' death, when all of His blood has been shed, is the moment when Divine Mercy is freely available to all mankind. That moment is recorded in the Gospel of John, but not in the Gospels of Matthew, Mark and Luke. Why? It is because John is the only evangelist who is an eyewitness and records the last shedding of the blood:

> "It was the Day of Preparation, and to avoid the bodies' remaining on the cross during the Sabbath—since that Sabbath was a day of special solemnity—the Jews asked Pilate to have the legs broken and the bodies taken away. [32] Consequently the soldiers came and broke the legs of the first man who had been crucified with him and then of the other. [33] When they came to Jesus, they saw he was already dead, and so instead of breaking his legs [34] *one of the soldiers pierced his side with a lance; and immediately there came out blood and water."* [288]

We know from reliable medical authorities that when the blood and water issued from the wound made by the lance, Jesus was already dead. Kenneth E. Stevenson and Gary R. Habermas write on page 141 of their book:

> *"All physicians who have examined the question agree that Jesus was already dead when the chest wound was inflicted."*[289]

---

286 *Catechism*, Article 1225

287 John 19: 34-35

288 John 19: 31-34

289 Kenneth E. Stevenson and Gary R. Habermas, *Verdict on the Shroud,* (Ann Arbor, MI: Servant Publications) 1981, p. 141

I would like to quote from the definitive documentation of Pierre Barbet, M.D., in his classic book: *A Doctor at Calvary*. The moment in John 19: 34 is described in chapter 7 which he titles "The wound in the heart," and he begins the chapter with these words:

> "I say "wound in the heart" and not wound in the side, because this is attested by tradition, and it has been confirmed for me by experiment. The blow of the lance which was given to the right side reached the right auricle of the heart, perforating the *pericardium*[290]." [291]

He concludes this chapter with the following statement:

> "Yes, John was certainly clear-sighted. What he saw as the blood from the auricle and the water from the pericardium. I also have seen them (in experiments), *et verum est testimonium meum.*[292] " [293]

We know that Scripture is the true word of God. But some need more proof, so we have bolstered John's witness status by medical documentation and experimentation.

The author of the Letter to the Hebrews puts it together for us this way:

> "We have then, brothers, complete confidence through the blood of Jesus in entering the sanctuary, [20] by a new way which he has opened for us, *a living opening through the curtain, that is to say, his flesh.* [21] And we have the high priest over all the sanctuary of God. [22] So as we go in, let us be sincere in heart and filled with faith, our hearts sprinkled and free from any trace of bad conscience, and our bodies washed with pure water." [294]

That *"living opening through the curtain, that is to say, his flesh,"* might just as well be rendered by a Torretto translation as:

> "We have then, brothers, complete confidence through the blood of Jesus in entering the sanctuary by a new way which he has opened

---

290 *Pericardium*: The membranous sac enclosing the heart.
291 Pierre Barbet, M.D., *A Doctor at Calvary* (Garden City, NY: Image Books) 1963, p. 129.
292 *"et verum est testimonium meum"* i.e., "and my testimony is true."
293 Barbet, *op. cit.*, p. 147
294 Hebrews 10: 19-22

for us, a living opening through the curtain, that is to say, *through the spear wound in His heart."*

Jesus confirms this for us when He tells St. Faustina:

"At three o'clock, implore My mercy, especially for sinners; and, if only for a brief moment, immerse yourself in My Passion, particularly in My abandonment at the moment of agony. *This is the hour of great mercy for the whole world.* **I will allow you to enter into My mortal sorrow. In this hour, I will refuse nothing to the soul that makes a request of Me in virtue of My Passion...."** [295]

This is the Hour of Great Mercy since Jesus gives an extraordinary promise of conversion for sinners at that hour when this prayer is uttered:

"Today Jesus said to me, **I desire that you know more profoundly the love that burns in My Heart for souls, and you will understand this when you meditate upon My Passion. Call upon My mercy on behalf of sinners; I desire their (93) salvation. When you say this prayer, with a contrite heart and with faith on behalf of some sinner, I will give him the grace of conversion. This is the prayer:**

"O Blood and Water, which gushed forth from the Heart of Jesus as a fount of Mercy for us, I trust in You." [296]

If that then, is the moment when Divine Mercy is for the first time freely available to all mankind, it is most appropriate for us to look for the first miracle of Divine Mercy at that moment.

The Synoptic evangelists all attest to major conversions at that moment. Matthew writes:

"And suddenly, the veil of the Sanctuary was torn in two from top to bottom, the earth quaked, the rocks were split, [52] the tombs opened and the bodies of many holy people rose from the dead, [53] and these, after his resurrection, came out of the tombs, entered the holy city and appeared to a number of people. [54] The centurion, together with the others guarding Jesus, had seen the earthquake and all that was

---

295 Dairy Entry 1320
296 Ibid., Entries 186-7

taking place, and they were terrified and said, 'In truth this man was son of God.'" [297]

Mark writes:

"And the veil of the Sanctuary was torn in two from top to bottom. [39] The centurion, who was standing in front of him, had seen how he had died, and he said, 'In truth this man was Son of God.'" [298]

And Luke writes:

"It was now about the sixth hour and the sun's light failed, so that darkness came over the whole land until the ninth hour. [45] The veil of the Sanctuary was torn right down the middle. [46] Jesus cried out in a loud voice saying, 'Father, into your hands I commit my spirit.' With these words he breathed his last. [47] When the centurion saw what had taken place, he gave praise to God and said, 'Truly, this was an upright man.'" [299]

The three Synoptics identify the major conversion was that of a centurion.

But John, the eyewitness, writes nothing about these conversions.

"After Jesus had taken the wine he said, 'It is fulfilled'; and bowing his head he gave up his spirit. [31] It was the Day of Preparation, and to avoid the bodies' remaining on the cross during the Sabbath—since that Sabbath was a day of special solemnity—the Jews asked Pilate to have the legs broken and the bodies taken away. [32] Consequently the soldiers came and broke the legs of the first man who had been crucified with him and then of the other. [33] When they came to Jesus, they saw he was already dead, and so instead of breaking his legs [34] one of the soldiers pierced his side with a lance; and immediately there came out blood and water. [35] This is the evidence of one who saw it—true evidence, and he knows that what he says is true—and he gives it so that you may believe as well. [36] Because all this happened to fulfil the words of scripture: Not one bone of his will be broken;

---

297 Matthew 27: 51-54
298 Mark 15: 38-39
299 Luke 23: 44-47

and again, in another place scripture says: They will look to the one whom they have pierced." [300]

This is where we must do some detective sleuthing. It is all there for us to find, but we just have to look with the eyes of faith to find the clues.

"we walk by faith and not by sight;" [301]

Matthew, Mark and Luke are *not* eyewitness and are obviously quoting something they have heard, been told or researched. We know Luke did his research. He tells us so in the beginning of his Gospel:

> "Seeing that many others have undertaken to draw up accounts of the events that have reached their fulfillment among us, [2] as these were handed down to us by those who from the outset were eyewitnesses and ministers of the word, [3] *I in my turn, after carefully going over the whole story from the beginning, have decided to write an ordered account for you,* Theophilus, [4] so that your Excellency may learn how well founded the teaching is that you have received." [302]

Although these conversions can be considered miracles of faith, I sense there is a *physical reason* why these miracles of faith took place. To do more detective sleuthing we must go to the other foundation of our Catholic Faith: *Tradition.*

We find that the name of the soldier who thrust the lance into Jesus' side comes to us from the apocryphal *Gospel of Nicodemus* formerly called *The Acts of Pontius Pilate*:

> "Then Longinus, a certain soldier, taking a spear, pierced his side, and presently there came forth blood and water." [303]

Later the *Gospel of Nicodemus* picks up on the Scripture words:

> "But when the centurion saw that Jesus thus crying out gave up the ghost, he glorified God, and said, 'Of a truth this was a just man.'" [304]

---

300 John 19: 30-37
301 2 Corinthians 5: 7
302 Luke 1: 1-4
303 *The Gospel of Nicodemus* 7: 8
304 *Ibid.,* 8: 5

Note these two quotations. The lance wound comes before Jesus' death in this account. This shows one reason why the *Gospel of Nicodemus* was not accepted into the official Church Canon of Scriptures.

But, this name of Longinus does enter into tradition as a legend. More information about Longinus is found in Blessed Jacobus de Voragine's, O.P., *The Golden Legend: Readings on the Saints*. It is dated from the thirteenth century. The opening lines read:

> "Longinus, which was a puissant knight, was with other knights, by the commandment of Pilate, on the side of the cross of our Lord, and pierced the side of our lord with a spear; and when he saw the miracles, how the sun lost his light, and great earthqaving (sic) of the earth was, when our Savior suffered death and passion in the tree of the cross, then believed he in Jesus Christ.

> *Some say that when he smote our Lord with the spear in the side, the precious blood traveled by the shaft of the spear upon his hands, and of adventure with his hands he touched his eyes, and anon he that had been tofore blind saw anon clearly,* wherefore he refused all chivalry and abode with the apostles, of whom he was taught and christened, and after, he abandoned them to lead an holy life in doing alms and in keeping the life of a monk about thirty-eight years in Caesarea and in Cappadocia, and by his word and his example many men converted he to the faith of Christ." [305]

There also is an early written tradition that comes from the Ethiopic Manuscript called *The Lament of the Virgin* dating from the 5th or 6th century. This tradition takes a different twist. It is the burial wrappings that are the source of healing:

> "And the centurion…seizing the wrappings…embraced them, and when they, touched his face he immediately saw with his blind eye as before, as if Jesus laid his hand on it as he had done with the blind man." [306]

---

305 Blessed Jacobus de Voragine's, O.P., *The Golden Legend: Readings on the Saints*, Section 47

306 *Mingana*, 1928. Christian documents in Syriac, Arabic, and Garshuni with two introductions by Rendel Harris. Woodbrooke Studies, Vol. 2. Cambridge: W. Heffer & Sons, p.206. (Reprinted from the Bulletin of the John Rylands Library, 5 Vol. 12, 1928),

Keeping in mind that these are legends, both legends have a physical healing as the basis for the conversion and faith in Jesus Christ. Both legends state the healing is of a blind eye.

But the Golden Legend has more ancillary things to support it and make it more credible.

It is possible that the blood and water coming forth from the side wound would be forceful enough to travel down the shaft of the spear into the Centurion's hands. However, the pressure would not come from a beating heart since Jesus is already dead.

However, it is more likely that the force from the released pressure in the heart cavity would spew the blood and water onto the face of the Centurion as he looked up to drive the lance into the Savior's side. Gary Habermas in his book, *Verdict on the Shroud,* which I quoted earlier, writes about his personal conversations with Dr. Robert Bucklin, the official pathologist on the Shroud of Turin Study (STURP). [307] He writes that the water came out *AS* from a punctured bag. With all the weight of the body now settling downwards since Jesus no longer was alive to lift himself up to breath, it would naturally create pressure in pericardial sac.

Jesus alludes to the force of the release of the Blood and Water from His side in the prayer He gives to St. Faustina:

"O Blood and Water, which *gushed* forth from the Heart of Jesus as a fount of Mercy for us, I trust in You." [308]

Let us do a little more sleuthing. John 19: 34 reads "immediately there came out blood and water." The words *"there came out"* in Greek, *exerchomai,* mean *to escape, as under pressure,* or *to spread abroad, or gush forth under pressure.* So "gushed" is an appropriate translation of John 19: 34.

Therefore, it is believable that the pressure release was of such a force that some of the Blood and Water literally sprinkled the face of the Centurion. His normal reflex would be to rub his eyes to clear them. Then in astonishment when he knew he could see clearly he would exclaim: *"Surely this was the Son of God."*

The legend is reinforced by the fact that the *"Breviarus"* states that in 570 the pilgrim St. Antonius of Piancenza describes the holy places of Jerusalem and that in the Basilica on Mount Zion he saw the crown of thorns and the *Lance of Longinus.*

There is the Syriac manuscript in the Laurentian Library at Florence, illuminated by Rabulas in 586, that has the name Longinus written in Greek

---

307 Habermas, *op.cit.*, p. 136.
308 Dairy Entry 187

characters (*Loginos*) over the head of the soldier thrusting the lance into the Savior's side.

There is a problem with the fact that *the* Lance would be in a shrine somewhere. Not that it wouldn't be revered, but how could one get a Roman Solider to part with his spear? He would be subject to capital punishment if he lost or gave away his weapon.

If it was a soldier who thrust the lance, then the Centurion who exclaimed *"'In truth this man was Son of God'"* could have ordered the soldier to part with his weapon.

And if it were the Centurion who thrust the lance, he would have to be convinced to part with his weapon. Now, who would have enough influence to convince him to do either?

Scripture gives the clue as to who might have that type of influence:

> "It was now evening, and since it was Preparation Day—that is, the day before the Sabbath— [43] there came Joseph of Arimathea, a prominent member of the Council, who himself lived in the hope of seeing the kingdom of God, and *he boldly went to Pilate and asked for the body of Jesus.* [44] Pilate, astonished that he should have died so soon, summoned the centurion and enquired if he had been dead for some time. [45] Having *been assured of this by the centurion,* he granted the corpse to Joseph [46] who bought a shroud, took Jesus down from the cross, wrapped him in the shroud and laid him in a tomb which had been hewn out of the rock. He then rolled a stone against the entrance to the tomb. [47] Mary of Magdala and Mary the mother of Joset took note of where he was laid." [309]

Any Jew who could *boldly* go to the Roman Procurator and request the body of a *criminal* has the influence we are looking for. Also note:

> "Pilate, astonished that he should have died so soon, summoned the centurion and enquired if he had been dead for some time.[45] *Having been assured of this by the centurion,* "

The centurion now knew Joseph of Arimathea's influence with Pilate, so he was probably easily convinced by Joseph of Arimathea to part with the Lance, most likely being promised by Joseph of Arimathea to replace it.

But why would Joseph of Arimathea want the lance? The reason isn't in the legend, but starts in scripture. To answer that we must do further detective sleuthing.

---

309 Mark 15: 42-47

Scripture says:

> "Take care, however, not to eat the blood, since blood is life, and you must not eat the life with the meat." [310]

We know from the rabbis that when someone dies violently or in a way which causes the spilling of blood, those who gather up the body must gather with it every piece of remains that contains blood. [311]

You can see this today in Israel when a suicide bomber leaves mangled bodies strewn about. There are teams of men scouring the area to gather each and every piece of material with blood on it and actually blotting the area to collect as much of the blood as possible to bury with the deceased.

And you might recall the scene from the *Passion of the Christ* by Mel Gibson that showed Mary on her knees wiping up with towels the blood of Jesus left from the Scourging.

Now because of the violent and traumatic death of Jesus all the artifacts that could be collected with blood would be gathered to be buried with him. But it would seem there is no scriptural reference to support that.

But there is in the Gospel of John:

> "So Peter set out with the other disciple to go to the tomb. [4] They ran together, but the other disciple, running faster than Peter, reached the tomb first; [5] he bent down and saw the linen cloths lying on the ground, but did not go in. [6] Simon Peter, following him, also came up, went into the tomb, saw the linen cloths lying on the ground [7] and also the cloth that had been over his head; this was not with the linen cloths but rolled up in a place by itself." [312]

The clue is in this line: *",,,and also the cloth that had been over his head; this was not with the linen cloths but rolled up in a place by itself."* The face cloth (*Sudarium*) covered the disfigured face from view until the burial cloth could be placed over the body. Then, instead of being discarded, since it had blood on it, it was placed in the tomb with the body.

That cloth, the *Sudarium*, is in the Cathedral of Oviedo, Spain, and is documented to have been there since the mid-7th century. [313] Tests have

---

310 Deuteronomy 12: 23

311 "Burial and Burial Customs," *The Universal Jewish Encyclopedia 2*, 1940: pp. 594-604.

312 John 20: 3-7

313 Mark Guscin, *The Oviedo Cloth* (Cambridge, England: The Lutterworth Press) 1998, pp. 11-15.

shown that, although the *Sudarium* does not have the imprint of the face of Jesus as does the Shroud of Turin, there are over 70 congruent blood stains on the front and over 50 congruent blood stains on the back of the *Sudarium* that match scientifically the wound marks and blood stains on the Shroud.[314]

Doctors Mary and Alan Whanger (devote Protestants) developed the Polarized Image Overlay Techniques to study the Shroud. They found the faint images of many items of the Passion *"shadowed"* on the Shroud, including the outline of a Roman *hasta*, or thrusting spear.[315]

Now that we know that the spear image may be on the Shroud of Turin, let us do some detective sleuthing about the Centurion who goes by the name Longinus.

Later details added to the Legend state that Gaius Cassius, *alias or a.k.a.* St. Longinus, was born in the Roman town called Anxanum (*an-zan-noom*), halfway between Loreto and San Giovanni Rotondo. He became a soldier, rising to the rank of centurion (a captain over 100 men). Eventually, he was sent to Judea as part of the Italian cohort mentioned in Acts:

> "One of the centurions of the Italian cohort stationed in Caesarea was called Cornelius." [316]

A Roman cohort contains 300 to 600 men. As you can see there were more than one centurion in a cohort and Cornelius and Longinus are two different men.

Pontius Pilate, the Procurator of Judea, resided most of the time in Caesarea Maritima. When he went to Jerusalem part of the Italian cohort traveled with him, since they were more trustworthy than the mercenaries.

In Roman writings it is not unusual to find that many soldiers were given the name Longinus because of their prowess or skill with their weapon.

After the Legend of St. Longinus grew in popularity the town of *Anxanum* changed its name to *Lanciano* (Italian meaning *"the Lance"*) in honor of its famous son. The Golden Legend (and variations) state the eventually Longinus, once converted, gave up his position in the Roman Army, was instructed by the Apostles, settled in Cappadocia and eventually died there as a martyr for his faith. To this day there is an altar in Basilica of the Holy Sepulcher dedicated to St. Longinus. Since 1257 it has been in the possession of the Franciscans.

Meanwhile back in Lanciano, the Greek Rite Monks of St. Basil

---

314 *Ibid.*, pp. 27-32.
315 Mary and Alan Whanger, *The Shroud of Turin* (Franklin, TN: Providence House Publishers) 1998, pp. 89-90.
316 Acts 10: 1

established a monastery under the patronage of St. Logontian (St. Longinus) and St. Domitian. In 700 a Basilian priest, with a crisis of faith concerning the real presence of Jesus in the Eucharist, was celebrating Mass with this lingering doubt. At the moment of Consecration, he prayed fervently to be released from this doubt.

As he elevated the Host, his hands began to tremble. Soon he realized what was happening and his whole body began to shake. He slowly turned to the congregation and said:

> "O fortunate witnesses to whom the Blessed God, to confound my disbelief, has wished to reveal himself in this Most Blessed Sacrament and to render Himself visible to our eyes. Come, brethren, and marvel at our God so close to us. Behold the Flesh and Blood of our most beloved Christ." [317]

The people dropped to their knees as they saw the Host had turned to flesh and the wine to Blood.

This would have been the end of the miracle *if* the Flesh and Blood had disintegrated following the laws of nature. Defying the physical laws of nature, the Flesh and Blood remain intact to this day, over 1300 years later.

Many tests have been performed on the Flesh and Blood; the most recent and most extensive in 1970-71 with the permission of Pope Paul VI. The results of the tests were:

- The flesh is real flesh and the blood is real blood.
- The flesh and blood belong to the human species
- The flesh consists of the muscular tissue of the heart (myocardium).
- The flesh and blood have the same blood type (AB).
- In the blood are proteins in the same normal proportions as found in the sero-proteic make up of fresh, normal blood.
- The blood contains other normal minerals.
- The preservation of the flesh and blood, which were left in their natural state for twelve centuries and were exposed to the action of atmospheric and biological agents, is without the trace of any materials or agents for the preservation of flesh, and remains an extraordinary phenomenon.

---

317 Excerpt from a document kept at Lanciano. Cf. *The Eucharistic Miracle of Lanciano, Italy,* Thérèse Tardif, quoted by www.michaeljournal.org/home.htm

Please note: the Shroud of Turin, the Sudarium, and the Eucharistic Miracle of Lanciano all have the same blood type: AB, from a male human.

This would have been just another Eucharistic Miracle except for fact that God is confirming the Legend of St. Longinus.

Notice, the flesh of the Lanciano Eucharistic Miracle is a very specific type of flesh. It is identified in the report as striated (grooved or ridged) muscular tissue of the myocardium (heart wall). Only a hand experienced in anatomic dissection could have obtained from a hollow internal organ, the heart, such an expert cut, made tangentially that is, a round cut, thick on the outer edges and lessening gradually and uniformly into nothingness in the central area.

> "He who created the stars and calls them by name has again shown us the work of His Hand." [318]

What we see is the God of All Truth showing us without a doubt that *the First Miracle of Divine Mercy* (the healing of the blind eye of the Centurion who thrust the Lance into the Heart of the Savior, opening up the Fount of Divine Mercy) *is confirmed by the First known Eucharistic Miracle* (a Host that turns into His heart wall tissue), in the hometown of the Centurion who thrust the spear into the Heart of the Savior opening up the Fount of Divine Mercy.

But to give added testimony to the First Miracle of Divine Mercy and the First Eucharistic Miracle, the miracle that is used for the Canonization of St. Faustina, the Secretary of Divine Mercy, is that of Jesus' healing Fr. Ron Pytel's heart.

Let us recall the circumstances of Fr. Ron Pytel's miracle.

Fr. Ron Pytel was the Pastor of Holy Rosary Church in Baltimore, Maryland. In 1995, during a bout with bronchitis he quickly got out of breath just climbing the stairs. An examination by the doctors showed a massive build-up of calcium in his aortic valve and the left ventricle badly damaged.

In June he had surgery to replace the damaged valve with an artificial one. His first regular check-up after that revealed severe damage to his heart.

He was told by a renowned cardiologist that his heart would never be normal and he would never likely resume his priestly duties although he was only 48 years old.

On October 5, 1995, the Feast day of St. Faustina, he attended a healing service and prayed that Sister Faustina intercede for him. He venerated the relic and then collapsed for 15 minutes.

---

318 cf. Psalm 8: 3

At his next check-up the doctor could not explain why Fr. Pytel's heart had returned to normal.

A panel of doctors in November 1999 declared the healing was scientifically unexplainable. The theologians of the Church's Congregation for the Causes of Saints declared it a miracle on December 7, 1995. December 14, a panel of cardinals and bishops gave their approval. On December 20, 1999, Pope John Paul II approved the healing as a miracle.

The miracle was the reason Sister Faustina was canonized on Mercy Sunday, April 30, 2000.

Please read Appendix D for Fr. Pytel's own testimony from his parish website.

Holy Scripture itself gives credence to our discovery of the First Miracle of Divine Mercy. Since God Himself verifies it with a Eucharistic Miracle of Heart Flesh at Lanciano, and the Miracle of Healing the Heart of Fr. Ron Pytel in Baltimore, Maryland.

Does not Scripture say?

> "A single witness will not suffice to convict anyone of a crime or offence of any kind; whatever the misdemeanor, the evidence of two witnesses or three is required to sustain the charge." [319]

And Jesus supports this saying in Matthew.

> "If he does not listen, take one or two others along with you: whatever the misdemeanor, the evidence of two or three witnesses is required to sustain the charge." [320]

We have our 2 or 3 witnesses.

Let us ask God to heal us of spiritual blindness like He healed St. Longinus of his physical blindness, and free us from our doubts about the Real Presence as He did for the Basilian Monk at Lanciano. Let us ask St. Faustina to help us to go deeply in the Heart of the Merciful Jesus and enter the Ocean of Mercy.

Each time we approach the Real Presence of Jesus in the Eucharist, knowing in it He is the Fount of all Mercy and the Source of all Truth, let us remember what we have learned here. Like St. Longinus let us ask God to heal us of spiritual blindness and our doubts about the Real Presence.

Let us end with St. Thomas Aquinas' prayer about the Real Presence: (*Adoro Te Devote*, translated by Fr. Gerard Manley Hopkins).

---

319 Deuteronomy 19: 15
320 Matthew 18: 16

"Godhead here in hiding, whom I do adore
Masked by these bare shadows, shape and nothing more,
See, Lord, at thy service low lies here a heart
Lost, all lost in wonder at the God thou art.

Seeing, touching, tasting are in thee deceived;
How says trusty hearing: that shall be believed;
What God's Son has told me, take for truth I do;
Truth himself speaks truly or there's nothing true."

Truth is Truth! Truth himself speaks truly or there's nothing true."

**"O Blood and Water, which gushed forth from the Heart of Jesus
as a fount of Mercy for us, I trust in You."** [321]

Saint Longinus, Pray for us

---

[321] Dairy Entry 187

Chapter 8

St. Luke: the Gospel of Mercy

Introduction to Chapter 8
St. Luke: the Gospel of Mercy

In 1998, I was asked by Dr. Robert Stackpole, The John Paul II Institute of Divine Mercy, to participate in the First North American scholarly symposium devoted to the theology of the Divine Mercy.

Dr. Stackpole asked me to consider presenting a theological essay to be titled "St. Luke, the Gospel of Mercy," from John Paul II's statement in his Encyclical: *"Dives in Misericordia,"* "The Gospel writer who particularly treats of these themes in Christ's teaching is Luke, whose Gospel has earned the title the *"Gospel of Mercy."* [322]

I accepted, of course, but it was later that I began to worry: I found out the quality of the other presenters. The list is staggering:

> Reverend George W. Kosicki, C.S.B.
> Dr. Robert Stackpole, STD
> Reverend Raymond Gawronski, S. J.
> Reverend Seraphim Michalenko, M.I.C., Vice Postulator for Sister
>   Faustina's canonization
> Reverend John Horgan, STL
> Dr. Mark Miravalle, STD

My essay is presented here as given at the symposium held in Washington, D.C., January 28-31, 1999.

Most of the theological essays have been published by The John Paul II Institute of Divine Mercy in their book: *Divine Mercy: The Heart of the Gospel,* edited by Robert Stackpole.

---

322   Pope John Paul II, *Dives in Misericordia,* (St. Paul Editions; Boston, MA) 1980, p. 13.

St. Luke: The Gospel of Mercy

Our past Supreme Pontiff, John Paul II, writing about the Mercy of God in his encyclical, *Dives in Misericordia*, makes this momentous statement concerning God's Mercy as one of the principal themes of Jesus' Messianic Message:

> "The Gospel writer who particularly treats of these themes in Christ's teaching is Luke, whose Gospel has earned the title of "The Gospel of Mercy." [323]

This statement by the Vicar of Christ, the chief Teacher of the Magisterium, who is guided by the same Holy Spirit Who inspired the Scripture writers, demands we study the Gospel of Luke with a new focus.

Although his statement should be a sufficient reason for us to re-study the Gospel of Luke, it receives additional emphasis when we understand that Saint Faustina as Secretary to the King of Mercy [324] records these words of Jesus in her Diary: ***"Write this: before I come as the just Judge, I am coming first as the King of Mercy..."*** [325] And again in her Diary: ***"You will prepare the world for My final coming,"*** [326] and, finally: ***"My hand is reluctant to take hold of the sword of justice. Before the Day of Justice I am sending the Day of Mercy."*** [327]

As we approach the Third Millennium I am not espousing that the End

---

323 Pope John Paul II, *Dives in Misericordia*, (St. Paul Editions; Boston, MA) 1980, p. 13.

324 Sister M. Faustina Kowalska, *Divine Mercy in My Soul, Diary*, (Stockbridge, MA: Marian Press) 1987, Entry 965

325 *Ibid.*, Entry 83

326 *Ibid.*, Entry 429.

327 *Ibid.*, Entry 1588.

Times are imminent. However, since I am approaching my 76th birthday, I clearly see my Day of Mercy as now, and my Day of Judgment approaching quickly. Therefore, I offer in this chapter a part of my study of the Gospel of Luke as the Gospel of Mercy.

As one reads the four Gospels it becomes readily apparent that Matthew, Mark and Luke resemble each other while the Gospel of John does not resemble the other three. The similarities of the three are known as the "Synoptic Problem." The similarities are so striking that when you read each of the three gospels it appears as if you are looking at the three with a one-eye focus. In a sense, nothing could be further from the truth. Just trying to make a synopsis of the three gospels as one gospel gives us more problems than it solves.

One attempt that seems more helpful than others is the work by Burton H. Throckmorton, Jr., *Gospel Parallels: A Synopsis of the First Three Gospels,* in which the gospels are published in an event sequence with these similarities written, side by side, or parallel, instead of sequential. [328]

This synoptic problem presents us with a *tool* for use in re-studying the Gospel of Mercy: there is a certain amount of material in Luke's Gospel that is unique to him and not found in Matthew or Mark. The amount of material can range wildly from 1/3 to over ½ of Luke's Gospel depending upon which scholar's proposal you choose to follow. I personally ascribe to just under ½ of Luke's Gospel material as unique to him (approximately 520 verses out of 1150). [329]

Why is this material so important to our re-studying of Luke? Luke's Gospel is the only Gospel composed in two parts: what we know as 1), the Gospel of Luke, and, 2), the Book of Acts. Luke is the only author[330] who tells us why he is writing, that he did his research, and that he was familiar with other authors, all which point to a methodical, scholarly prepared presentation following an orderly plan.

Luke begins his work with these words:

"Seeing that many others have undertaken to draw up accounts of the events that have reached their fulfillment among us, as these were handed down to us by those who from the outset were eyewitnesses

328 Burton H. Throckmorton, Jr., *Gospel Parallels: A Synopsis of the First Three Gospels,* (New York, NY: Thomas Nelson, Inc.) 1973.

329 Raymond E. Brown, S. S., Joseph A. Fitzmyer, S. J., Roland E. Murphy, O. Carm., Editors, *The Jerome Biblical Commentary,* Volume II, "Synoptic Problem," (Englewood Cliffs, NJ: Prentice-Hall, Inc.) 1968, p. 2.

330 The Gospel of St. John does allude to the author's purpose at the end of the Gospel (John 20: 30-31)

and ministers of the word. I in my turn, after carefully going over the whole story from the beginning, have decided to write an ordered account for you, Theophilus, so that your Excellency may learn how well founded the teaching is that you have received." [331]

In the second part of his Gospel, Acts, Luke gives emphasis to his original plan:

"In my earlier work, Theophilus, I dealt with everything Jesus had done and taught from the beginning until the day he gave his instructions to the apostles he had chosen through the Holy Spirit, and was taken up to heaven." [332]

Therefore, our *tool* for the restudy is to look at the material unique to Luke in order to find out why the Gospel of Luke is the Gospel of Mercy.

Since Luke is a Greek physician, he should be very fluent with the Greek language. In fact, his opening statement to Theophilus in Luke 1: 1-4 uses a classical vocabulary and follows the literary construction style of contemporary Greek historians. [333] Then we should not be surprised if Luke uses the Septuagint (LXX, the Greek translation of the Hebrew Scriptures) for research and citations. *The Dictionary of Jesus and the Gospels* states:

"The OT (i.e., the LXX) plays a very important role in this Gospel. The Evangelist not only cites specific passages and alludes to many others, he borrows its vocabulary and imitates its style." [334]

One of the vocabulary words Luke borrows from the Septuagint is the Greek word used to translate the Hebrew *hesed* (2617).[335] Pope John Paul II alludes to Luke's adoption of the OT meaning of *hesed* in His mercy parables in Luke 15. Commenting in *Dives in Misericordia* the Pontiff writes:

"The father's fidelity to himself—a trait already known by the Old

---

331 Luke 1: 1-4

332 Acts 1: 1-2

333 *The New Jerusalem Bible,* footnote *a,* p. 1687.

334 Joel B. Green, Scot McKnight, I. Howard Marshall, Editors, *Dictionary of Jesus and the Gospels,* "Old Testament in the Gospels," (Downers Grove, IL: Intervarsity Press) 1992, p. 586.

335 Numbers in parentheses after Hebrew and Greek words are from *Strong's Exhaustive Concordance of the Bible.*

Testament term hesed—is at the same time expressed in a manner particularly charged with affection."[336]

Because John Paul II's comment includes the entire Old Testament, one might draw the conclusion that the word *hesed* (חסד) is the word most often used in the Hebrew Scriptures for the Mercy of God.

Therefore, let us determine what GREEK word is used to commonly translate *hesed* (חסד) into the Greek Septuagint version of the Old Testament that St. Luke used.

From an Old Testament verse quoted in the New Testament we find that the Greek word *eleos* (ελεοσ) (1656) is generally used to translate the Hebrew word *hesed* (חסד). We seem to have identified our key word. Using a good concordance we can find the verses where the Greek word *eleos* (ελεοσ) is used within the material unique to the Gospel of Luke.

Once we have the locations of these words they become for us a series of dots. If we connect the dots then we should have a road map for the direction of Luke's use of the word mercy as a theme of the Messianic Message. It would seem we have our answer.

However, a quick review shows more than 80% of the verses unique to Luke do not contain a word identified as translating the Old Testament concept of *hesed* (חסד) or Mercy!

Although many scripture commentators have accepted this premise and only address Divine Mercy in the context of *hesed* (חסד) I propose that this does not solve any of our problems with translations and meanings. But rather, the quick acceptance of this Hebrew word *hesed* (חסד) as a *word for word* translation of Divine Mercy limits and clouds our understanding and keeps us from a deeper understanding of God's Mercy.

Let me restate this. If St. Luke's Gospel is the Gospel of Mercy, it is not because he uses one Greek word *eleos* (ελεοσ) for the Hebrew *hesed* (חסד) for mercy, much more often, nor in more unique passages than do the other Gospel writers. [337]

A key question we need to ask ourselves at this point is this: "Why does Luke consciously use these unique verses if *NOT* for a word for word translation of *eleos* (ελεοσ) for *hesed*?"

---

336 Pope John Paul II, *op. cit.*, p. 21.

337 A key to what Luke understood and avoided begins to become apparent with this quote:
"In the LXX the noun *eleos* is normally used for the Hebrew *hesed* which has to do with the attitude of a human or a God arising out of a mutual relationship... Less frequently (six times), *eleos*, is used in the LXX for the Hebrew *rahaamin* (as is *oiktirmoi*, etc.)," Green, McKnight, Marshall, *op. cit.*, pp. 541-542

I propose that Scripture commentators today have lost sight of a basic translation problem that Luke understood immediately as he did his study and research in planning and compiling his Gospel.

A quick check in any concordance will show that there are others words in Hebrew that are used to convey the concept of Mercy. Of course we have *hesed* (chesed) (חסד) (2617) which means *kindness, pity* or *mercy*. It comes from the root word *chacad* (חסד) (2616) which means *to bow the neck (only) in courtesy to an equal, to be kind* or *merciful*. There is *chanan* (חנן) (2603) a prime root word which means *to bend or stoop in kindness to an inferior, to have pity on, or be merciful*. There is *racham* (רחם) (7356) which means compassion or mercy and comes from the word *racham* (רחם) (7355) a prime root which means *to fondle as a child, to be compassionate or have mercy*.

Another Hebrew word, which comes from this prime root, gives a nuance to mercy that is truly unfathomable to a Western mind. The Hebrew word *rechem* (רחם) (7358) also from *racham* (7356) (רחם) *Rechem* (רחם) (7358) is the Hebrew word for the womb of a woman. Our Hebrew ancestors understood the opening of the womb of a woman and giving new life as a Divine Act of Mercy.

> "Sons are a birthright from Yahweh, children are a reward from him…" [338]

As an aside let me say this: we have just had the anniversary of Roe versus Wade (January 22). The whole Right to Life and Right to Abortion issue can be summed up in the great difference between Semitic thinking (right brain) and Greek thinking (left brain). And I believe this nuance is not lost on Luke, the Physician!

Our Semitic, Eastern or Oriental, spiritual ancestors, the Jews, used the same root word for expressions of the gift of life and compassion or mercy: *rechem* and *racham*; for them the gift of life outweighs the pain of childbirth. However, our Occidental or Western, philosophical and linguistic ancestors, the Greeks, viewed it not so much a gift as a burden. Note that our English noun, *Hysteria* and our English adjective, *hysterical*, come from the Latin word, *hystericus,* which is derived from *hustera,* the Greek word for the womb. The Oriental or Eastern mind looks at the womb as giving the *gift* of life and mercy: the Occidental or Western mind looks at the womb and birth as a burden filled with screams and trauma. My vote is with the Jews!

Let me return to my focus on the Gospel of Luke.

There are some basic rules of translation that merit reiteration at this point.

---

338 Psalm 127: 3

No. 1 It is impossible to do a word for word translation of a language that is accurate to the author's original meaning. Nuances in meaning are unique to a particular language and preclude an accurate rending of the original meaning in the second language. That is why there are so many different translations of the Bible available. Father Lukefahr writes:

"Some translations follow the original language quite closely, while freer translations, or 'paraphrases' (such as *The Living Bible),* reword and restate ideas. The first approach can provide a version that faithfully presents the thought of the original author, but the language maybe stilted. The second approach might have the advantage of producing a more readable text, but it can also impose a translator's biases on the content." [339]

No. 2 Translating from Hebrew to Greek (Old Testament to New Testament) presents even greater challenges to the translator.

a. Hebrew is sometimes called a poverty language, meaning it has a very small vocabulary.
b. Hebrew has no adjectives.
c. In Hebrew there are only two tenses (verbal time forms). [340]
d. Whereas, the six tenses of the Greek verb are more numerous than those of other languages; and each verb also has five Moods.
e. Hebrew has no subordinate clauses. (The more subordinate clauses or modifiers the narrower and more specific the meaning.)
f. Hebrew is a "concrete" language, i.e., very direct, forward, and earthy. [341]

---

339 Father Oscar Lukefahr, C.M., *A Catholic Guide to the Bible,* (Liguori, MO: Liguori Press, 1992), p. 11.

340 The two tenses are: 1} A perfect tense used for the present tense, and, 2} An imperfect tense used both for the imperfect and the future. (If a prophet writes using this tense there is a translator's problem to determine whether he means the past or the future.

341 "This concept is fully justified and supported by the countless acknowledgments of Bible translators as to the inadequacy of the customary method. Martin Luther, whose translation of the Hebrew Scriptures into German in AD 1534 "spiritualized Germany and made the German language," stated it plainly: "The words of the Hebrew tongue have a peculiar energy. It is impossible to convey so much so briefly in any other language. To render them intelligibly we must not attempt to give word for word

g. Greek tends to be "expansive," definitive, and abstract.

Therefore, Hebrew, a concrete, direct, earthy language with a simple grammatical structure and limited vocabulary must necessarily have more nuances to a given word than an expansive, vocabulary rich and grammatically complex language like Greek. *Shalom*, peace, might have as many nuances to it as *Aloha* does in Hawaiian. Fr. Richard Murphy in his book *Background to the Bible* writes:

> "Despite its drawbacks, the Hebrew language can be highly praised and appreciated even by non-linguists. It is a concrete language, very direct and sometimes earthy. The very poverty of the language—its relatively small vocabulary – means that some words have layers and layers of meaning. A good example of this is the word hesed, long translated "loving kindness" or "steadfast love." Actually hesed is a covenant word, implying a relationship that is more personal than legal, a bond of loyalty. *The Jerusalem Bible* translates the word as "tenderness;" it is all that, and more (see Hosea 2: 21, 4:2; y6: 6). Another good example is the word "knowledge." To us knowledge means information, but the Hebrew knowledge of God was "covenant-oriented" – a "knowledge" of the heart. The Hebrew "knows" God as he "knows" his wife – with a deep personal understanding and love…" [342]

Therefore, we need to take another look at the Gospel passages unique to Luke and find what is in them that helps to give depth of meaning to Divine Mercy. Mercy is not just a word for Luke, but a concept with many layers of meaning, presented in many ways.

The first thing that we notice is the Infancy Narratives. Matthew also has an Infancy Narrative. But Luke's narratives deal with the details of the births allowing for an expansion of our understanding of the momentousness of the events. Luke begins with the birth of John the Baptist, who is a bridge between the Old and New Testaments.

Although that is significant, the major point is that Elizabeth has been barren, to the Jews a sign of God's disfavor, since there is no fruit of her womb given by God.

---

translations, but only aim at the sense and the (original Author's) idea." (Table Talk). *The Amplified Bible*, "Publisher's Foreword," (Grand Rapids MI: Zondervan Bible Publishers, 1965).

342   Richard T. A. Murphy, O. P., *Background to the Bible*, (Ann Arbor, MI: Servant Books, 1978), p. 150.

We should immediately call to mind the Hebrew word for Mercy that fits this situation, "*Racham*," and its sister word, *Rechem*, or "womb," which conveys powerful emotion because the fruit of the womb is of God's gift of life.

Mary understands the full significance of this favor from God and goes immediately to celebrate it with Elizabeth. It is Elizabeth who recognizes not only her own favor from God, but the grace bestowed on Mary and exclaims:

'Of all women you are the most blessed, and blessed is the fruit of your womb." [343]

Next we notice there are three pieces of poetry in Luke's Infancy Narratives. They are not found anywhere else. So powerful are these pieces of poetry, it has been the tradition of the Catholic Church since the time of St. Benedict, the Father of Western Monasticism, that these canticles serve as the great daily hymns of the Liturgy of the Hours. The *Benedictus* of Zachary recited daily at Lauds; the *Magnificat* of the Blessed Virgin at Vespers, and the *Nunc Dimittis* of Simeon at Compline.

But for our purposes it is worth noting that each one deals with Mercy and Faithfulness. Both the *Benedictus* and the *Magnificat* have the Greek word *Eleos* for *Hesed* (or Mercy) and the *Nunc Dimittis* refers to the faithfulness of God in fulfilling not only His promise to Simeon, but also to His people Israel, by sending his Salvation.

Some Scripture scholars have shown that St. Luke uses a literary device in the canticles called "poetic *parallelism.*" [344] "*Poetic Parallelism*" *is a peculiarity of Hebrew poetry. Fr. Murphy writes this about poetic* parallelism:

"...Hebrew poetry never employed rhyme, but is governed instead by the laws of parallelism. This means that Hebrew poetry matches ideas instead of words. The ideas are matched and balanced, set off one against the other: half-line against half-line; verse against verse; or groups of verses against other groups of verses. Once the reader has

---

343 Luke 1: 42

344 "There are both resemblances and differences if we compare the canticles among themselves. By way of resemblances they are all highly suggestive of OT and intertestamental passages…, almost to the point that one can speak of them as mosaics pieced together with OT pieces. Yet the poetic patterns vary, with much closer poetic parallelism being found in the Magnificat than in the Benedictus." Raymond E. Brown, S. S., *The Birth of the Messiah*, (Garden City, NY: Doubleday, 1977), p. 348.

begun to notice this pattern he will begin to appreciate the artistry involved. Parallelism is extremely ingenious, and is no doubt more difficult to work out in practice than to describe after the fact." [345]

There are different types of poetic parallelism [346] employed by Hebrew Poetry. For example:

1. *Synonymous parallelism:* it occurs when the same idea is set forth twice in different words. We see this in the *Magnificat:*

"My *soul proclaims the greatness of the Lord* [first time] and my *spirit rejoices in God my Saviour* [second time]. [347]

2. *Antithetic parallelism:* it occurs when things are stated in opposition or contrast. We see this also in the *Magnificat:*

"He has *pulled down the princes* from their *thrones* and *raised high the lowly.* He has filled the starving with good things, sent the rich away empty." [348]

The point is, since the idea of *hesed* (Mercy) is proclaimed in both the *Benedictus* and *Magnificat*, by using *Poetic Parallelism*, Luke is not only able to expand the meaning of the nuances of Divine Mercy through the juxtaposition of ideas so common in poetry, but also to repeat ideas, balance them, and define them by their negative opposite by the means of the poetic parallelism. Luke is able to condense so much more meaning in so little written space.

Moreover, Luke being the non-Jew, a foreigner, is conscious that God's salvation is for all mankind. So Luke uses a literary construct that gives meaning to the universality of Divine Mercy. In explaining the Mission of John the Baptist, Luke quotes the Prophet Isaiah just as Matthew does. However, Luke expands and finishes his quote from Isaiah by adding verse 5 from Isaiah 40:

---

345 Richard T. A. Murphy, O. P., *op. cit.*, p. 36.
346 Also *synthetic parallelism* occurs when the second part of the verse is used to combine, expand, develop or explain the thought of the first part. This form is difficult to explain and demonstrate in this paper, but will be the subject of any additional expansion of these ideas for restudy.
347 Luke 1: 46-47
348 Luke 1: 52-53.

"...and all humanity will see the salvation of God." [349]

Then to further emphasize that God's Salvation and Mercy is for all mankind, Luke presents the genealogy of Jesus. Unlike Matthew's genealogy, which begins with Abraham, the Father of the Jews, Luke goes back to Adam, *the father of all mankind*. Luke ends his genealogy by these words"...son of Adam, son of God," identifying God as Adam's Father.

Therefore, Luke is saying all descendants of Adam are "children of God," thus giving Jesus' mission of Divine Mercy a universal character. In a unique twist Luke shows Mary in the royal family lineage descending from David through one of his other sons, Nathan. It is the origin of the genealogy from God and Mary's lineage that makes Luke's genealogy unique and different from Matthew's by making God's Mercy and His Salvation universal and inclusive. This is confirmed by Jesus' words to Sr. Faustina in the Diary:

> Today the Lord said to me, **My daughter, My pleasure and delight, nothing will stop Me from granting you graces. Your misery does not hinder My Mercy. My daughter, write that the greater the misery of a soul, the greater its right to My mercy; [urge] all souls to trust in the unfathomable abyss of My mercy, because I want to save them all. On the cross, the fountain of My mercy was opened wide by the lance for all souls – no one have I excluded!** [350]

Having established the universality of Divine Mercy and Salvation, Luke continues to confirm this by his use of incidents and parables that are unique to his Gospel. For Luke, Jesus is the Savior of all people. To emphasize this, his narrative includes every gender, class and moral character conceivable. Just within the material unique to Luke we find:

- The cure of the Centurion's servant. *A military man from the Occupation force.*
- A son raised to life because he is *the only son of a widow who would be left destitute.*
- *A woman of questionable reputation* who anoints Him.
- Woman companions, *considered second class citizens*, who traveled with his group and ministered to them and supported them out of their own purse. [351]

---

349 Luke 3: 5.
350 Diary, Entry 1182
351 Luke 8: 1-3

- Cure of demoniac, *perhaps a psychologically-mentally handicapped person.* (I prefer what St. Luke, the doctor, writes: *"a man possessed."*)
- The Good Samaritan: *a heretical sectarian half-breed.*
- Stayed with apparently *unattached woman* in her house (*Martha*)
- Praised an unjust and crafty steward.
- *Homeless poor/sick man (Lazarus)* is shown to gain heaven and God's love and mercy.
- Cure of lepers, *medical/sectarian outcasts.*
- Publican praised/ Pharisee put down *(politically correct ideas turned upside down)*
- Dined with *outcast tax collector,* Zacchaeus
- Asks forgiveness for those who crucify Him (*His enemies*).

Each of these people is a complete outsider either socially or religiously. The Kingdom of God, God's Divine Mercy, is freely given to each as gift. The only thing that stops them from accepting the gift of God is their own refusal to repent and seek forgiveness. We find this paramount because it is only Luke who specifically enumerates this in his unique material:

> "[1a] It was just about this time that some people arrived and told him about the Galileans whose blood Pilate had mingled with that of their sacrifices. [2] [1b] At this he said to them, [2] 'Do you suppose that these Galileans were worse sinners than any others, that this should have happened to them? [3] They were not, I tell
> you. No; but unless you repent you will all perish as they did. [4] Or those eighteen on whom the tower at Siloam fell, killing them all? Do you suppose that they were more guilty than all the other people living in Jerusalem? [5] They were not, I tell you. No; but unless you repent you will all perish as they did.' [6] He told this parable, 'A man had a fig tree planted in his vineyard, and he came looking for fruit on it but found none. [7] He said to his vinedresser, "For three years now I have been coming to look for fruit on this fig tree and finding none. Cut it down: why should it be taking up the ground?" [8] "Sir," the man replied, "leave it one more year and give me time to dig round it and manure it: [9] it may bear fruit next year; if not, then you can cut it down." [352]

Less we miss this point, Luke reiterates this in his summary of Jesus

---

352 Luke 13: 1-9

fulfillment of His Mission and His commissioning of His disciples. And this material is unique to Luke:

"...and he said to them, 'So it is written that the Christ would suffer and on the third day rise from the dead, [47] and that, in his name, repentance for the forgiveness of sins would be preached to *all nations*, beginning from Jerusalem. [48] You are witnesses to this. [49] 'And now I am sending upon you what the Father has promised. Stay in the city, then, until you are clothed with the power from on high.'" [353]

Notice Luke does not use the phrase "the good news," but rather "repentance for the forgiveness of sins"! What a striking difference! In order to be forgiven you have to acknowledge you are a sinner.

Remember forgiveness is open to all those who acknowledge that they need it. Jesus confirms this:

Write this for the benefit of distressed souls: *when a soul sees and realizes the gravity of its sins*, when the whole abyss of the misery into which it immersed itself is displayed before it eyes, let it not despair, but with trust let it throw itself into the arms of My mercy, as a child into the arms of it beloved mother. These souls (125) have a right a priority to My *compassionate Heart, they have first access to My mercy*. Tell them that no soul that has called upon My mercy has been disappointed or brought to shame. I delight particularly in a soul which has placed its trust in My goodness." [354]

Continuing in the material unique to Luke we find some parables and some incidents which are only found in Luke. Everyone knows that Jesus talked in parables. But not everyone knows that parables are not unique to Jesus.

If parables are not unique to Jesus why does Luke include so many that Matthew and Mark do not? Does the fact that he positions the majority before and after chapter 13, which deals with *repentance* hold significance for us? It would therefore seem appropriate to refresh our understanding of exactly what a parable is. *The Dictionary of Jesus and the Gospels* presents this information:

"The English word parable refers to a short narrative with two levels of meaning... Parables tend to be brief and symbolical. They often make

---

353 Luke 24: 46-49
354 Diary, Entry 1541

use of balanced structures involving two or three movements. The typically omit unnecessary descriptions and frequently leave motives unexplained and implied questions unanswered..." [355]

That a parable might have multi-levels of meaning and that it is the hearer who must draw conclusions and make decisions are very important. For Divine Mercy or Salvation is a gift of God for all mankind and requires a real decision for us to receive and accept it. In the Diary we have a description of Jesus working with a sinful soul:

"...Jesus calls to the soul a third time, but the soul remains deaf and blind, hardened and despairing. Then the mercy of God begins to exert itself, and, without any co-operation from the soul, God grants it final grace. *If this too is spurned, God will leave the soul in this self-chosen disposition for eternity.* This grace emerges from the merciful Heart of Jesus and gives the soul a special light by means of which the soul begins to understand (83) God's effort; but conversion depends on its own will. The soul knows that this, for her, is final grace and, should it *show even a flicker of good will*, the mercy of God will accomplish the rest..." [356]

When he first uses a parable by Jesus, Luke makes sure that we understand the need for us to listen in order to enter into the meaning of the parable: not to be deaf, but to understand, perceive, and respond to it:

"And some seed fell into good soil and grew and produced its crop a hundredfold.' Saying this he cried, 'Anyone who has ears for listening should listen!' 9] His disciples asked him what this parable might mean, [10] and he said, 'To you is granted to understand the secrets of the kingdom of God; for the rest it remains in parables, so that they may look but not perceive, listen but not understand."[357]

The parables selected by Luke have more than one level of meaning and yet they have a simplicity, which allows the hearer, who, listens, to enter into them easily, making personal judgments and decisions very quickly. [358]

The parables that I will use to end this brief attempt at restudying the

---

355 Joel B. Green, Scot McKinght, I. Howard Marshall, *op. cit.*, pp. 591-4.
356 Diary, Entry 1486
357 Luke 8: 8-10
358 Then Luke reinforces our need to follow this path by gathering parables according to their complementary nuances.

Gospel of Luke as the Gospel of Mercy are so powerful, that most Bibles will subtitle the parables that begin Luke 15 as "Three Parables of God's Mercy." They are so well known that just using a key word from each is sufficient to make everyone sit up and respond "I know that one." Feel your own response to these key words: "The Lost Sheep." "The Lost Coin." "The Prodigal Son." You have already made an emotional response to them. Why? Because they strike an emotional chord in everyone.

No one wants to feel lost. Everyone wants to feel special. Therefore, if we have a God that will leave 99 good sheep to find one lost one and you are the lost one, don't you feel wanted and special? If God will not be just satisfied with what coins remain, but will look for the one lost coin to make his treasure complete again, don't you feel special and wanted? Commenting on the parables in Luke 15,

> "The great liberal Jewish scholar C. G. Montefiore held strongly that this is the one absolutely new thing which Jesus came to say. The idea of a God who will invite the sinner back is not new; the idea of a God who will welcome back the penitent sinner is not new; *but the idea of a God who will go and seek for the sinner, and who wants men to do the same, is something completely new.* Montefiore would find the very center and soul and essence of the Christian Gospel in Luke 15: 1-10, in the story of the shepherd searching for the lost sheep and the woman searching for the lost coin." [359]

Therefore Rabbi Montefiore writes:

> "The picture in the Gospels both of what Jesus did, and the society among which he moved, was not merely invented. It is in its main features historic. And the saying of Jesus in 17 aptly and historically describes a most important part of his character and ministry. He sought to bring back into glad communion with God those whom sin, whether 'moral' or ceremonial," had driven away. For him sinners (at least certain types of sinners) were the subject not of condemnation or disdain, but of pity. He did not avoid sinners, *he sought them out.* They were still children of God. This was new and sublime contribution to the development of religion and morality... To deny the greatness and originality of Jesus in this connection, to deny that he opened a new

---

359   William Barclay, *The Apostles' Creed for Everyman,* New York: Harper & Row, 1967), p. 47.

chapter in men's attitude to sin and sinners is, I think to beat the head against the wall." [360]

Later, commenting on Luke 15: 1, Montefiore makes this comment:

"This verse sums up one of the specific characteristics of Jesus and one of the new excellences of the gospel. 'The sinners drew near to hear him.' Surely this is a new note, something which we have not yet heard in the Old Testament or of *its* heroes, something which we do not hear in the Talmud or of *its* heroes. 'The sinners drew near to hear him': his teaching did not repel them. It did not palter with, or make light of sin, but yet it gave comfort to the sinner. The virtues of repentance are gloriously praised in the Rabbinical literature, but this direct search for, and appeal to, the sinner are new and moving notes of high import and significance.'" [361]

Luke understands this. Therefore, in chapter 19, Jesus stays at the home of the tax collector, Zacchaeus, whose conversion takes place. And as He leaves to finish His ascent to Jerusalem and the completion of His mission given by the Father we read:

"...And Jesus said to him, 'Today salvation has come to this house, because this man too is a son of Abraham; [10] for the Son of man has *come to seek out and save what was lost.*'" [362]

This quote recalls to mind what is written in Luke 15: 6 ("and then, when he got home, call together his friends and neighbours, saying to them, "Rejoice with me, I have found my sheep that was lost."), and Luke 15: 9 ("And then, when she had found it, call together her friends and neighbours, saying to them, "Rejoice with me, I have found the drachma I lost.") and Luke 15: 24 ("because this son of mine was dead and has come back to life; he was lost and is found." And they began to celebrate.") and Luke 15: 32 ("But it was only right we should celebrate and rejoice, because your brother here was dead and has come to life; he was lost and is found.'")

This is a God who finds each soul special and will leave everything to find it. Jesus reiterates that he seeks out sinners:

---

360 Montefiore, C. G., *The Synoptic Gospels*, Volume I, (New York: KTAV Publishing House, 1968), p. 55.

361 Montefiore, C. G., *The Synoptic Gospels*, Volume II, (New York: KTAV Publishing House, 1968)

362 Luke 19: 9-10

"(90) Write: I am Thrice Holy, and I detest the smallest sin. I cannot love a soul which is stained with sin; but when it repents, there is no limit to My generosity toward it. My mercy embraces and justifies it. With My mercy, *I pursue sinners along all their paths*, and My Heart rejoices when they return to Me. I forget the bitterness with which they fed My Heart and rejoice at their return..." [363]

And in the Diary Sr. Faustina relates a conversation of the Merciful God with a despairing soul:

"The mercy of God, hidden in the Blessed Sacrament, the voice of the Lord who speaks to us from the throne of mercy: **Come to Me, all of you.**

Conversation of the Merciful God with a Sinful Soul.

Jesus: **Be not afraid of your Savior, O sinful soul. I make the first move to come to you, for I know that by yourself you are unable to lift yourself to me. Child, do not run away from your Father; be willing to talk openly with your God of mercy who wants to speak words of pardon and lavish his graces on you. How dear your soul is to Me! I have inscribed your name upon My hand; you are engraved as a deep wound in My Heart.**

Soul: Lord, I hear your voice calling me to turn back from the path of sin, but I have neither the strength nor the courage to do so.

Jesus: **I am your strength, I will help you in the struggle.**

Soul: Lord, I recognize your holiness, and I fear you.

Jesus: **My child, do you fear the God of mercy? My holiness (80) does not prevent Me from being merciful. Behold, for you I have established a throne of mercy on the earth—the tabernacle— and from this throne I desire to enter into your heart. I am not surrounded by a retinue or guards. You can come to me at any moment, at any time; I want to speak to you and desire to grant you grace.**

---

363 Diary, Entry 1728

Soul: Lord, I doubt that You will pardon my numerous sins; my misery fills me with fright.

Jesus: **My mercy is greater than your sins and those of the entire world. Who can measure the extent of my goodness? For you I descended from heaven to earth; for you I allowed myself to be nailed to the cross; for you I let my Sacred Heart be pierced with a lance, thus opening wide the source of mercy for you. Come then, with trust to draw graces from this fountain. I never reject a contrite heart. Your misery has disappeared in the depths of My mercy. Do not argue with Me about your wretchedness. You will give me pleasure if you hand over to me all your troubles and grieves. I shall heap upon you the treasure of My grace...** [364]

Notice the action of the Shepherd when he finds the lost sheep,

"And when he found it, would he not joyfully take it on his shoulders" [365]

and compare this action to what Jesus says in the diary:

"...Jesus: **What joy fills My Heart when you return to me. Because you are weak, I take you in My arms and carry you to the home of My Father..."** [366]

I would like to end by giving some comments on the parable of the Prodigal Son. There has been so much written about this parable that is saccharine and is what I term "sloppy *agape*." However, in our study of St. Luke's Gospel as the Gospel of Mercy, there are several points that need to be made about this parable.

No one would question the statement that this parable is really about the Mercy and Compassion of God the Father as John Paul II so elegantly stated in the opening quotation of this paper:

"The Gospel writer who particularly treats of these themes in Christ's

---

364 Ibid., Entry 1485
365 Luke 15:5
366 *Ibid.*, Entry 1486

teaching is Luke, whose Gospel has earned the title of "The Gospel of Mercy." [367]

Notice that the Father gives the son freedom to make his own choices and that when the son responds to circumstances and begins to repent, this statement in Luke is most important for two reasons. Here are the verses:

> "Then *he came to his senses* and said, "How many of my father's hired men have all the food they want and more, and here am I dying of hunger! [18] *I will leave this place and go to my father* and say: Father, I have sinned against heaven and against you; [19] I no longer deserve to be called your son; treat me as one of your hired men." [20] So he left the place and went back to his father. [368]

The verse: *"I will leave this place and go to my Father"* is important in our study of Divine Mercy because it states that our destination is not a place, Heaven, but a person, God the Father. Once we realize this, our response to the Good News becomes overwhelmingly personal. Jesus emphasizes this:

> "…Jesus: **What joy fills My Heart when you return to me. Because you are weak, I take you in My arms and carry you to the home of My Father…**" [369]

During the whole time the son is gone, the Father waits and longs for his return, eager to get him back. That personal love and longing with thorough respect for the free will of the son is mirrored the diary when Jesus says to Sr. Faustina:

> "**…Tell sinners** *that I am always waiting for them*, **that I listen intently to the beating of their heart. when will it beat for Me? Write, that** *I am speaking to them through their remorse of conscience, through their failures and sufferings,* **through thunderstorms, through the voice of the Church…**" [370]

Jesus seeks, waits, cajoles, encourages, and even turns our failures and sufferings into messages from Him to get us to return, repent and receive His Mercy. And it is all a personal, loving, compassion that causes Him to

367 Pope John Paul II, *op. cit.*, p. 13
368 Luke 15: 17-19
369 Diary, Entry 1486
370 *Ibid.*, Entry 1728

act the way He does. We forget that the Trinity is Persons and we need to understand that the concept of Person is really a Christian Concept. Pagan philosophers never developed a concept of person. But the early Fathers alluded to the concept and the Scholastics developed a very rich doctrine with many positions. [371]

One of the most important things about a human person is that he or she possesses personalities and emotions. Relating to the Father is different from relating to the Son, and to the Holy Spirit. Jesus throughout the Diary expresses His response and actions in emotional and personal terms. We tend to respond too quickly to His ANGER, but overlook the depths and nuances of His Love. And His Love is very emotional.

I believe the reason the parable of the Prodigal Son is embedded in the memory of so many Christians is precisely because it is so personal and emotional. Even though the English translations do not do justice to the nuances in the Greek which come from the Hebrew, each of us have an innate spiritual perception that there is more depth to the Father's response then we can read in the English text. This is absolutely true.

When I covered the four different Hebrew words from Mercy and their Greek counterparts, I purposely avoided one Greek word for compassion and mercy which first shows up in Luke:

> "...because of the faithful love of our God in which the rising Sun has come from on high to visit us..."[372]

This is the next to the last line in the *Benedictus*. Some translations will use mercy here. The Greek phrase translated as one word is *"splagchna eleous."* Of course, *eleous* is a form of eleos which I have discussed, but the word *"splagchna"* (4697) adds a nuance of meaning in the Greek that is rarely conveyed for us in English. Literally translated, *splagchna eleous, "through the bowels of mercy."* Our Puritanical ears are offended by this gross phrase. But we must understand that to the Jews the bowels were the center of all the

---

371 "The best pagan philosophy (e.g., Aristotle) never explored fully the problem of person. The concept of 'person' is almost exclusively Christian, for it developed in the light of the mysteries of the Trinity and the Incarnation. These mysteries suggested the distinction between nature and person, which was the first conquest of Christian thought. The Scholastics (St. Thomas, *Summa Theologiae*, I, q. 29, a. 1-2), following in the step s of the Fathers, elaborated a rich doctrine with varied positions." Pietro Parante, Antonio Piolanti, Salvatore Garofalo, *Dictionary of Dogmatic Theology*, (Milwaukee, WI: Bruce Publishing, 1951), p. 215.

372 Luke 1: 78

emotions of the human being. It is the realm of the gut that we don't show to others.

Here Zechariah, his voice restored, tells us of the emotional love, compassion and Mercy God the Father has for us. He has opened the womb of his barren wife, and sends him as a herald for the Messiah, the King of Mercy!

Commenting on this, *The Dictionary of Jesus and the Gospels* says this:

"In Luke 1: 78 he employs the striking phrase *splagchna eleous*, "bowels of mercy." *Splagchna* expresses the idea of "feelings" (see 2.1.2 below); the genitive *eleous* is one of kind: the kind of feelings God has are merciful. The thought has moved from *hesed* (in so far as there is a distinction of meaning) to *rahamim*... The Greek verb is *splagchnizomai* (cf. The noun *splagchna* above) which, like the Hebrew *rahamim* (which the noun translates in Proverbs 12: 10), denotes a feeling that is felt physically, an emotion. Literally, *splagchnizomai* means 'to be moved in one's bowels.' The Greeks regarded the bowels as the seat of violent passion such as anger and love; the Jews regarded them as the center of the more tender affections, especially kindness and pity." [373]

When we come to the parable of The Prodigal Son, no matter what English translation you use it falls short of the emotional expression in the Greek text.

I now give you several translations of Luke 15: 20:

"...But while he was at a distance, his father saw him and had compassion, and ran and embraced him and kissed him." (*Revised Standard Version*)

"...But when he was yet a great way off, his father saw him, and had compassion, and ran, and fell on his neck, and kissed him." (*King James Version*)

"...But while he was still far off, his father saw him and was filled with compassion; he ran and put his arms around him and kissed him." (*The New Revised Standard Version*)

"...So he got up and went back to his father. While he was still a long way off, his father caught sight of him, and was filled with compassion.

373   Green, McKnight, Marshall, *op. cit.*, p. 542.

He ran to his son, embraced him and kissed him. "(*New American Bible*)

"...'While he was still a long way off, his father saw him and was moved with pity. He ran to the boy, clasped him in his arms and kissed him." (*The New Jerusalem Bible*)

Only the NRSV and NAB with their use of *"filled with compassion"*, and NJB with its use of *"was moved with pity,"* give hints that there might be more emotion here than we read in the English. And there is so much more in the Greek that is not translated here.

The father of the prodigal is moved in his bowels with pity *"splagchna eleous"* for his son. Added emphasis is given by the description that the father kissed him. Against something is lost in the translation. The Greek word, *kataphileo* (2705), usually translated as kissed, is a combination of two words, *kata* (2596), and *phileo* (5368). *Kata* used as a prefix to a word frequently denotes intensity or feverishness, which again gives credence to the emotional nuances of the father's actions. [374] "He showered kisses on him" would be a good idiomatic translation.

Jesus is giving us His personal comment about His Father's mercy, compassion and love for us. Since Jesus says to Philip in the Final Discourse in the Gospel of John:

"[8b] Jesus said to him, [9] 'Have I been with you all this time, Philip, and you still do not know me?'Anyone who has seen me has seen the Father, so how can you say, "Show us the Father"? [375]

Let me say that Jesus confirms this in many Diary entries. But I will this entry:

"Write this: Everything that exists is enclosed in the bowels of My mercy, more deeply than an infant in its mother's womb. How painfully distrust of My goodness wounds Me! Sins of distrust wound Me most painfully. [376]

We begin to see that there is greater depth to St. Luke as the Gospel of Mercy than appears at the surface of most translations.

---

374 *Kataphileo* is used to describe the kissing with weeping done by the woman who washes Jesus' feet in Luke 7: 36-50.

375 John 14:9

376 Diary, Entry 1076

My purpose in presently this study is to challenge us to realize that *God feels and has strong, very strong emotions about His Children.* I believe a continued study of the Gospel of Luke as the Gospel of Mercy will help all of us to become more aware of God's deep emotional love for us. Once we realize that in our hearts, instead of our heads, we in turn might be *moved in our bowels* to respond in a deep emotional love for Our Father.

What do we do now? Where do we go from here? Do we continue this study? I believe the first step in answering these rhetorical questions is to be found in one of the earliest entries in Sr. Faustina's *Diary.* I offer it as a prayerful consideration for you and me:

> "Once I was at a dance [probably in Lodz] with one of my sisters. While everybody was having a good time, my soul was experiencing deep torments. As I began to dance, I suddenly saw Jesus at my side, Jesus racked with pain, stripped of His clothing, all covered with wounds, who spoke these words to me: **How long shall I put up with you and how long will you keep putting Me off?** At that moment the charming music stopped, [and] the company I was with vanished from my sight; there remained Jesus and I. I took a seat by my dear sister, pretending to have a headache in order to cover up what took place in my soul. After a while I slipped out unnoticed, leaving my sister and all my companions behind, and made my way to the Cathedral of Saint Stanislaus Kostka. It was already beginning to grow light; there were only a few people in the cathedral. Paying no attention to what was happening around me, I fell prostrate before the Blessed Sacrament and begged the Lord to be good enough to give me to understand what I should do next. [377]

---

377 *Ibid.*, Entry 9

Afterword

As I complete the last review of this manuscript I marvel at how I became involved with Divine Mercy, how in prayer I received the topics to research and teach, and how books and materials would become available as I needed them.

It is obvious the Hand of God has been directing this work!

I was born of Italian immigrants, the fifth of six children. When I began grammar school they stopped talking Italian to me so I would become "an American." I am the only sibling to go on to college and acquire a bachelor's degree.

While in High School I thought I had a vocation to become a priest and a teacher. So I joined the religious order that taught me: The Clerics of St. Viator, a French order from Canada.

Once I entered college they directed me into the study of languages. I received courses in German, French and Greek. I already had Latin from my Catholic grade and high schools.

Once I left the religious community I was subject to the Draft and began my Army career. Most of my assignments were as a teacher or administrator of teachers.

While stationed at the Pentagon in Washington, DC, I was told to begin a Masters Degree. I was the Protocol Officer to the Chief of Staff of the Army, so I entered The American College and received a Masters Degree in Public Relations and Journalism.

After an assignment in Europe I returned to the United States hoping to retire. Again the Army intervened and I was assigned to The Command and General Staff College, Leavenworth, Kansas as a teacher and then staff director of a teaching division.

While there I was introduced to Saint Mary College and the Sisters of Charity of Leavenworth. It was now that I became more active in my Church.

My final Army assignment was as the Professor of Military Science, St. Mary's University, San Antonio, Texas. I felt I needed to get a Masters in Theology. Again a language became a part of my studies: Hebrew.

My retirement brought me back to the Sisters of Charity of Leavenworth and Saint Mary College. I was their GED teacher in the State Penitentiary and then Director of their college program in the Federal Penitentiary, Leavenworth.

Introduced to the Charismatic Movement I became a teacher for it. While in prayer I received the topics to teach and then I would receive a call from a retired nun at Saint Mary College telling me she had a shipment of old library books that might be useful to me. At first I was surprised that they covered the topics I was going to teach. Later I would expect a call from her as I announced my topics for the year and would find the books I needed, many out of print.

During this time I was introduced to the Chaplet of Divine Mercy, but only the prayers.

My first association with any large conference on Divine Mercy was as the emcee of the first San Francisco conference. Being on or near the stage at all times I was immersed in talks and presentations on Divine Mercy. I did a presentation during the conference, but it was on Spiritual Warfare. It was well received and I was called back the next year to be a presenter of a Divine Mercy topic and my research began in earnest.

Several conferences later I was on the same platform with Dr. Robert Stackpole from the John Paul II Institute of Divine Mercy. My relationship with him and the Institute solidified. Many chapters in this book are the result of my presentations for the Institute.

After the Divine Mercy On-Site Seminar to Poland and Lithuania I was diagnosed with cancer. During the treatment I called the Institute to get a copy of the Original Vilnius Image of Divine Mercy. At the time I only owned a Hyla image. Fr. Seraphim told me that I could only get the Vilnius Image from Life Foundation Ministries in Bernalillo, New Mexico.

Elizabeth Hackett answered my phone call and I explained who I was and what I wanted. Her response was a question: "Are you the Rick Torretto that did the talk on the Chaplet of Divine Mercy at the Houston Conference?" "Yes," was my answer. Then she said, "I was listening to the tape of your talk when you called." Our close relationship began at that moment and continues today. In fact, we only live 20 minutes from each other in New Mexico.

Life Foundation Ministries uses three images in their ministry: the Shroud of Turin, the Image of Our Lady of Guadalupe, and the Vilnius Image of Divine Mercy.

Asked to be a presenter and researcher for them I began my studies of the images of the Shroud of Turin and Our Lady of Guadalupe and their relationship to the Vilnius Image of Divine Mercy.

My knowledge of Latin, Greek and Hebrew and the Scriptures all came into focus during my research and studies on Divine Mercy.

Chapter 3, What is Mercy, owes much to my Old Testament studies and my knowledge of Hebrew. Chapter 5, The Image of Divine Mercy and Chapter 6, The Novena and the Feast of Divine Mercy also draw on my scripture knowledge and my Hebrew which allows me to read and study the Rabbis' writings on the Old Testament. Chapter 8, St. Luke: the Gospel of Divine Mercy is a tour de force in which Latin, Greek, Hebrew and the Scriptures all come together. Chapter 7, The First Miracle of Divine Mercy, flows from my knowledge of Scripture, Church History, the Theology of the Eucharist and the Shroud of Turin. Chapter 4, The Chaplet of Divine Mercy, includes my studies of The Catechism of the Catholic Church, liturgy, the Theology of the Eucharist, Latin and Greek.

This resource is not the sum of my output, nor does it represent the end of my research, studies and talks.

I am available for retreats, seminars, missions and teachings. All are scripture based and faithful to the Magisterium.

I can be reached at:

Solomon's Court
P.O. Box 44144
Rio Rancho, NM 87174-4144
www.solomonscourt.com
solomonscourt@aol.com

Appendix A
Apostolic Penitentiary Decree

Introduction to Appendix A
Apostolic Penitentiary Decree

On June 29, 2002, the Holy See promulgated a decree creating new indulgences that may be gained by the faithful in connection with Divine Mercy Sunday (the Second Sunday of Easter).

The decree grants a plenary indulgence to those who fulfill all the conditions established, and a partial indulgence to those who incompletely fulfill the conditions.

The plenary indulgence is granted under the usual conditions (sacramental confession, Eucharistic communion and prayer for the intentions of Supreme Pontiff) to the faithful who, on the Second Sunday of Easter or Divine Mercy Sunday, in any church or chapel, with a spirit of complete detached from the affection for sin, even a venial sin, take part in the prayers and devotions held in honor of Divine Mercy or who, in the presence of the Blessed Sacrament exposed or reserved in the tabernacle, recite the Our Father and the Creed, adding a devout prayer to the merciful Lord Jesus (e.g. Merciful Jesus, I trust in you!).

Additional provisions are given for those who are impeded from fulfilling these requirements, but wish to acquire the plenary indulgence.

Additionally, the decree requires parish priests to inform the faithful of the Church's salutary provision. They should promptly and generously be willing to hear their confessions. On Divine Mercy Sunday, after celebrating Mass or Vespers, or during devotions in honor they should lead the recitation of the prayers given in the decree. When they instruct their people, priests should gently encourage the faithful to practice works of charity or mercy as often as they can.

Appendix A
Apostolic Penitentiary
Decree[378]

Indulgences attached to devotions in honour of Divine Mercy

"O God, your mercy knows no bounds and the treasure of your goodness is infinite..." (Prayer after the "Te Deum" Hymn) and "O God, you reveal your almighty power above all by showing mercy and forgiveness..." (Prayer for the 26th Sunday of Ordinary Time), in these prayers Holy Mother Church humbly and faithfully sings of Divine Mercy. Indeed, God's great patience with the human race in general and with each individual person shines out in a special way when sins and moral failures are forgiven by Almighty God Himself and the guilty are readmitted in a father like way to his friendship, which they deservedly lost.

Duty of honouring Divine Mercy

The faithful with deep spiritual affection are drawn to commemorate the mysteries of divine pardon and to celebrate them devoutly. They clearly understand the supreme benefit, indeed the duty, that the People of God have to praise Divine Mercy with special prayers and, at the same time, they realize that by gratefully performing the works required and satisfying the necessary conditions, they can obtain spiritual benefits that derive from the Treasury

---

378 www.vatican.va/roman_curia/tribunals/apost_penit/documents/rc_tri b_appen_doc_20020629_decree-ii_en.html

of the Church. "The paschal mystery is the culmination of this revealing and effecting of mercy, which is able to justify man, to restore justice in the sense of that salvific order which God willed from the beginning in man, and through man, in the world" (Encyclical Letter *Dives in misericordia*, n. 7).

It is God's Mercy that grants supernatural sorrow and resolution to amend Indeed, Divine Mercy knows how to pardon even the most serious sins, and in doing so it moves the faithful to perceive a supernatural, not merely psychological, sorrow for their sins so that, ever with the help of divine grace, they may make a firm resolution not to sin any more. Such spiritual dispositions undeniably follow upon the forgiveness of mortal sin when the faithful fruitfully receive the sacrament of Penance or repent of their sin with an act of perfect charity and perfect contrition, with the resolution to receive the Sacrament of Penance as soon as they can. Indeed, Our Lord Jesus Christ teaches us in the parable of the Prodigal Son that the sinner must confess his misery to God saying: "Father I have sinned against heaven and against you; I am no longer worthy to be called your son" (Luke 15, 18-19), realizing that this is a work of God, "for [he] was dead, and is alive; he was lost, and is found" (Luke 15, 32).

Second Sunday of Easter, Divine Mercy Sunday

And so with provident pastoral sensitivity and in order to impress deeply on the souls of the faithful these precepts and teachings of the Christian faith, the Supreme Pontiff, John Paul II, moved by the consideration of the Father of Mercy, has willed that the Second Sunday of Easter be dedicated to recalling with special devotion these gifts of grace and gave this Sunday the name, "Divine Mercy Sunday" (Congregation for Divine Worship and the Discipline of the Sacraments, Decree *Misericors et miserator*, 5 May 2000).

The Gospel of the Second Sunday of Easter narrates the wonderful things Christ the Lord accomplished on the day of the Resurrection during his first public appearance: "On the evening of that day, the first day of the week, the doors being shut where the disciples were, for fear of the Jews, Jesus came and stood among them and said to them, "Peace be with you'. When he said this, he showed them his hands and his side. Then the disciples were glad to see the Lord. Jesus said to them again, "Peace be with you. As the Father has sent me, even so I send you'. And then he breathed on them, and said to them, "Receive the Holy Spirit. If you forgive the sins of any, they are forgiven; if you retain the sins of any, they are retained'" (John 20, 19-23).

Plenary Indulgence

To ensure that the faithful would observe this day with intense devotion, the Supreme Pontiff himself established that this Sunday be enriched by a plenary indulgence, as will be explained below, so that the faithful might receive in great abundance the gift of the consolation of the Holy Spirit. In this way, they can foster a growing love for God and for their neighbour, and after they have obtained God's pardon, they in turn might be persuaded to show a prompt pardon to their brothers and sisters.

Pardon of others who sin against us

Thus the faithful will more closely conform to the spirit of the Gospel, receiving in their hearts the renewal that the Second Vatican Council explained and introduced: "Mindful of the words of the Lord: "By this all men will know that you are my disciples, if you have love for one another' (John 13, 35), Christians can yearn for nothing more ardently than to serve the men of this age with an ever growing generosity and success.... It is the Father's will that we should recognize Christ our brother in the persons of all men and love them with an effective love, in word and indeed (Pastoral Constitution, *Gaudium et spes*, n. 93).

Three conditions for the plenary indulgence

And so the Supreme Pontiff, motivated by an ardent desire to foster in Christians this devotion to Divine Mercy as much as possible in the hope of offering great spiritual fruit to the faithful, in the Audience granted on 13 June 2002, to those Responsible for the Apostolic Penitentiary, granted the following Indulgences:

A plenary indulgence, granted under the usual conditions (sacramental confession, Eucharistic communion and prayer for the intentions of Supreme Pontiff) to the faithful who, on the Second Sunday of Easter or Divine Mercy Sunday, in any church or chapel, in a spirit that is completely detached from the affection for a sin, even a venial sin, take part in the prayers and devotions held in honour of Divine Mercy, or who, in the presence of the Blessed Sacrament exposed or reserved in the tabernacle, recite the Our Father and the Creed, adding a devout prayer to the merciful Lord Jesus (e.g. Merciful Jesus, I trust in you!");

A partial indulgence, granted to the faithful who, at least with a contrite heart, pray to the merciful Lord Jesus a legitimately approved invocation.

For those who cannot go to church or the seriously ill

In addition, sailors working on the vast expanse of the sea; the countless brothers and sisters, whom the disasters of war, political events, local violence and other such causes have been driven out of their homeland; the sick and those who nurse them, and all who for a just cause cannot leave their homes or who carry out an activity for the community which cannot be postponed, may obtain a plenary indulgence on Divine Mercy Sunday, if totally detesting any sin, as has been said before, and with the intention of fulfilling as soon as possible the three usual conditions, will recite the Our Father and the Creed before a devout image of Our Merciful Lord Jesus and, in addition, pray a devout invocation to the Merciful Lord Jesus (e.g. Merciful Jesus, I trust in you).

If it is impossible that people do even this, on the same day they may obtain the Plenary Indulgence if with a spiritual intention they are united with those carrying out the prescribed practice for obtaining the Indulgence in the usual way and offer to the Merciful Lord a prayer and the sufferings of their illness and the difficulties of their lives, with the resolution to accomplish as soon as possible the three conditions prescribed to obtain the plenary indulgence.

Duty of priests: Inform parishioners,
hear confessions, lead prayers.

Priests who exercise pastoral ministry, especially parish priests, should inform the faithful in the most suitable way of the Church's salutary provision. They should promptly and generously be willing to hear their confessions. On Divine Mercy Sunday, after celebrating Mass or Vespers, or during devotions in honour of Divine Mercy, with the dignity that is in accord with the rite, they should lead the recitation of the prayers that have been given above. Finally, since "Blessed are the merciful, for they shall obtain mercy" (Mt 5, 7), when they instruct their people, priests should gently encourage the faithful to practice works of charity or mercy as often as they can, following the example of, and in obeying the commandment of Jesus Christ, as is listed for the second general concession of indulgence in the "Enchiridion Ingulgentiarum".

This Decree has perpetual force, any provision to the contrary notwithstanding.

Archbishop Luigi De Magistris,
Tit. Archbishop of Nova
Major Pro-Penitentiary
Fr Gianfranco Girotti, O.F.M. Conv.,
Regent

Appendix B
Proclamation of Divine Mercy Sunday

Introduction to Appendix B
Proclamation of Divine Mercy Sunday

On the Second Sunday of Easter of the Jubilee Year 2000, at the Mass for the Canonization of St. Faustina Kowalska, Pope John Paul II proclaimed to the world that "from now on throughout the Church" this Sunday will be called "Divine Mercy Sunday."

Many of the Church's faithful including pastors and liturgists were surprised by this announcement. Some wondered if this were a new feast.

To be sure, the Holy Father was well aware that the visions of Christ received by St. Faustina, and the messages and devotions coming from them, remain in the category of private revelations.

It is also true that the Church's doctrine of Divine Mercy, and her liturgical practices are not based on private revelations: they are based on Holy Scripture, the faith handed down by the apostles, and on liturgical traditions rooted in the worship life of the ancient, apostolic communities.

Indeed, the Second Sunday of Easter was already a solemnity as the Octave Day of Easter; nevertheless, the title "Divine Mercy Sunday" highlights the meaning of the day reflected in a teaching attributed to St. Augustine about the Easter Octave, which he called "the days of mercy and pardon," and the Octave Day itself "the compendium of the days of mercy."

Appendix B
Proclamation of Divine Mercy Sunday[379]

By virtue of a Decree issued on May 5, 2000 by the Congregation for Divine Worship and the Discipline of the Sacraments, the Holy See proclaimed the Second Sunday of Easter also as Divine Mercy Sunday.

Decree

Merciful and gracious is the Lord (Ps. 111:4), who, out of great love with which He loved us (Eph. 2:4) and [out of] unspeakable goodness, gave us his Only-begotten Son as our Redeemer, so that through the Death and Resurrection of this Son He might open the way to eternal life for the human race, and that the adopted children who received his mercy within his temple might lift up his praise to the ends of the earth.

In our times, the Christian faithful in many parts of the world wish to praise the divine mercy in divine worship, particularly in the celebration of the Paschal Mystery, in which God's loving kindness especially shines forth.

Acceding to these wishes, the Supreme Pontiff John Paul II has graciously determined that in the Roman Missal, after the title "Second Sunday of Easter," there shall henceforth be added the appellation "(or *Divine Mercy Sunday*)", and has prescribed that the texts assigned for that day in the same Missal and the Liturgy of the Hours of the Roman Rite are always to be used for the liturgical celebration of this Sunday.

---

379 http://www.zenit.org/article-9861?l=english

The Congregation for Divine Worship and the Discipline of the Sacraments now publishes these decisions of the Supreme Pontiff so that they may take effect.

Anything to the contrary notwithstanding.

Cardinal Jorge A. Medina Esteves

Prefect
+Francesco Pio Tamburrino

Archbishop Secretary

Appendix C
Novena to the Divine Mercy

Introduction to Appendix C
Novena to the Divine Mercy

Jesus instructed St. Faustina to write a Novena to the Divine Mercy and to recite it before the Feast of the Divine Mercy (Second Sunday of Easter). The Novena consisting of Chaplets to the Divine Mercy would begin on Good Friday. Each day has a particular intention to be prayed followed by one Chaplet.

In her diary, St. Faustina wrote that Jesus told her:

"…On each day of the novena you will bring to My Heart a different group of souls and you will immerse them in this ocean of My mercy.… On each day you will beg My Father, on the strength of My passion, for the graces for these souls." (Diary Entry 1209)

"…By this novena I will grant every possible grace to souls." (Diary Entry 796)

Appendix C
Novena to the Divine Mercy

It is recommended that the following novena intentions and prayers be said together with the Chaplet of Divine Mercy, since Our Lord specifically asked for a novena of Chaplets, especially before the Feast of Mercy.

(Diary Entries 1209-1230)[380]

Jesus, I trust in You.

Novena to The Divine Mercy which Jesus instructed me to write down and make before the Feast of Mercy. It begins on Good Friday.

I desire that during these nine days you bring souls to the fountain of My mercy, that they may draw there from strength and refreshment and whatever grace they need in the hardships of life, and especially at the hour of death.

On each day you will bring to My Heart a different group of souls, and you will immerse them in this ocean of My mercy, and I will bring all these souls into the house of My Father. You will do this in this life and in the next. I will deny nothing to any soul whom you will bring to the fount of My mercy. On each day you will beg My Father, on the strength of My bitter Passion, for graces for these souls.

---

380 Sister M. Faustina Kowalska, *Divine Mercy in My Soul, Diary,* (Stockbridge, MA: Marian Press) 1987, Diary Entries 1209-1230.

I answered, "Jesus, I do not know how to make this novena or which souls to bring first into Your Most Compassionate Heart." Jesus replied that He would tell me which souls to bring each day into His Heart.

First Day

Today, bring to Me all mankind, especially all sinners, and immerse them in the ocean of My mercy. In this way you will console Me in the bitter grief into which the loss of souls plunges Me.

Most Merciful Jesus, whose very nature it is to have compassion on us and to forgive us, do not look upon our sins but upon our trust which (58) we place in Your infinite goodness. Receive us all into the abode of Your Most Compassionate Heart, and never let us escape from it. We beg this of You by Your love which unites You to the Father and the Holy Spirit.

Oh omnipotence of Divine Mercy,
Salvation of sinful people,
You are a sea of mercy and compassion;
You aid those who entreat You with humility.

Eternal Father, turn Your merciful gaze upon all mankind and especially upon poor sinners, all enfolded in the Most Compassionate Heart of Jesus. For the sake of His sorrowful Passion, show us Your mercy, that we may praise the omnipotence of Your mercy for ever and ever. Amen.

Second Day

Today bring to me the souls of priests and religious, and immerse them in My unfathomable mercy. It was they who gave Me the strength to endure My bitter Passion. Through them, as through channels, My mercy flows out upon mankind.

Most Merciful Jesus, from whom comes all that is good, increase Your grace in us, that we may perform worthy works of mercy; and that all who see them may glorify the Father of Mercy who is in heaven.

The fountain of God's love
Dwells in pure hearts,
Bathed in the Sea of Mercy
Radiant as stars, bright as the dawn.

Eternal Father, turn Your merciful gaze (59) upon the company [of chosen ones] in Your vineyard — upon the souls of priests and religious; and endow them with the strength of Your blessing. For the love of the Heart of Your Son in which they are enfolded, impart to them Your power and light, that they may be able to guide others in the way of salvation and with one voice sing praise to Your boundless mercy for ages without end. Amen.

Third Day

Today bring to Me all devout and faithful souls, and immerse them in the ocean of My mercy. These souls brought Me consolation on the Way of the Cross. They were that drop of consolation in the midst of an ocean of bitterness.

Most Merciful Jesus, from the treasury of Your mercy You impart Your graces in great abundance to each and all. Receive us into the abode of Your Most Compassionate Heart and never let us escape from it. We beg this of You by that most wondrous love for the heavenly Father with which Your Heart burns so fiercely.

> The miracles of mercy are impenetrable.
> Neither the sinner nor just one will fathom them.
> When You cast upon us an eye of pity,
> You draw us all closer to Your love.

Eternal Father, turn Your merciful gaze upon faithful souls, as upon the inheritance of Your Son. For the sake of His sorrowful Passion, grant them Your blessing and surround them with Your constant protection. Thus may they never fail in love or lose the treasure of the holy faith, but rather, with all the hosts of Angels and Saints, may they glorify your boundless mercy for endless ages. Amen.

Fourth Day

Today bring to Me the pagans and those who do not yet know me. I was thinking also of them during My bitter Passion, and their future zeal comforted My Heart. Immerse them in the ocean of My mercy.

Most compassionate Jesus, You are the Light of the whole world. Receive into the abode of Your Most Compassionate Heart the souls of pagans who as yet do not know You. Let the rays of Your grace enlighten them that they, too, together with us, may extol Your wonderful mercy; and do not let them escape from the abode which is Your Most Compassionate Heart.

> May the light of Your love
> Enlighten the souls in darkness;
> Grant that these souls will know You
> And, together with us, praise Your mercy.

Eternal Father, turn Your merciful gaze upon the souls of pagans and of those who as yet do not know You, but who are enclosed in the Most Compassionate Heart of Jesus. Draw them to the light of the Gospel. These souls do not know what great happiness it is to love You. Grant that they, too, may extol the generosity of Your mercy for endless ages. Amen.

Fifth Day

Today bring to Me the souls of heretics and schismatics, and immerse them in the ocean of My mercy. During My bitter Passion they tore at My Body and Heart; that is, My Church. As they return to unity with the Church, My wounds heal, and in this way they alleviate My Passion.

Most Merciful Jesus, Goodness Itself, You do not refuse light to those who seek it of You. Receive into the abode of Your Most Compassionate Heart the souls of heretics and schismatics. Draw them by Your light into the unity of the Church, and do not let them escape from the abode of Your Most Compassionate Heart; but bring it about that they, too, come to glorify the generosity of Your mercy.

> (61) Even for those who have torn the garment of your unity,
> A fount of mercy flows from Your Heart.
> The omnipotence of Your mercy, Oh God.
> Can lead these souls also out of error.

Eternal Father, turn Your merciful gaze upon the souls of heretics and schismatics, who have squandered Your blessings and misused Your graces by obstinately persisting in their errors. Do not look upon their errors, but upon the love of Your own Son and upon His bitter Passion, which He underwent for their sake, since they, too, are enclosed in the Most Compassionate Heart of Jesus. Bring it about that they also may glorify Your great mercy for endless ages. Amen.

Sixth Day

Today bring to me the meek and humble souls and the souls of little children, and immerse them in My mercy. These souls most closely resemble My Heart. They strengthened Me during My bitter agony. I saw them as earthly Angels, who would keep vigil at My altars. I pour out upon them whole torrents of grace. Only the humble soul is able to receive My grace. I favor humble souls with My confidence.

62) Most Merciful Jesus, You yourself have said, "Learn from Me for I am meek and humble of heart." Receive into the abode of Your Most Compassionate Heart all meek and humble souls and the souls of little children. These souls send all heaven into ecstasy and they are the heavenly Father's favorites. They are a sweet-smelling bouquet before the throne of God; God himself takes delight in their fragrance. These souls have a permanent abode in Your Most Compassionate Heart, O Jesus, and they unceasingly sing out a hymn of love and mercy.

A truly gentle and humble soul
Already here on earth the air of paradise breathes,
And in the fragrance of her humble heart
The Creator Himself delights.

Eternal Father, turn Your merciful gaze upon meek souls, upon humble souls, and upon the souls of little children who are enfolded in the abode which is the Most Compassionate Heart of Jesus. These souls bear the closest resemblance to Your Son. Their fragrance rises from the earth and reaches Your very throne. Father of mercy and of all goodness, I beg You by the love You bear these souls and by the delight You take in them: Bless the whole world, that all souls together may sing out the praises of Your mercy for endless ages. Amen.

Seventh Day

Today bring to me the souls who especially venerate and glorify My mercy, and immerse them in My mercy. These souls sorrowed most over My Passion and entered most deeply into My Spirit. They are living images of My Compassionate Heart. These souls will shine with a special brightness in the next life. Not one of them will go into the fire of hell. I shall particularly defend each one of them at the hour of death.

63) Most Merciful Jesus, whose Heart is Love Itself, receive into the abode

of Your Most Compassionate Heart the souls of those who particularly extol and venerate the greatness of Your mercy. These souls are mighty with the very power of God Himself. In the midst of all afflictions and adversities they go forward, confident of Your mercy. These souls are united to Jesus and carry all mankind on their shoulders. These souls will not be judged severely, but Your mercy will embrace them as they depart from this life.

> A soul who praises the goodness of her Lord
> Is especially loved by Him.
> She is always close to the living fountain
> And draws graces from Mercy Divine.

Eternal Father, turn Your merciful gaze upon the souls who glorify and venerate Your greatest attribute, that of Your fathomless mercy, and who are enclosed in the Most Compassionate Heart of Jesus. These souls are a living Gospel; their hands are full of deeds of mercy, and their spirit, overflowing with joy, sings a canticle of mercy to You, O Most High! I beg You O God: Show them Your mercy according to the hope and trust they have placed in You. Let there be accomplished in them the promise of Jesus, who said to them, I Myself will defend as My own glory, during their lifetime, and especially at the hour of their death, those souls who will venerate My fathomless mercy.

Eighth Day

Today bring to Me the souls who are in the prison of Purgatory, and immerse them in the abyss of My mercy. Let the torrents of My Blood cool down their scorching flames. All these souls are greatly loved by Me. They are making retribution to My justice. It is in your power to bring them relief. Draw all the indulgences from the treasury (64) of My Church and offer them on their behalf. Oh, if you only knew the torments they suffer, you would continually offer for them the alms of the spirit and pay off their debt to My justice.

Most Merciful Jesus, You Yourself have said that You desire mercy; so I bring into the abode of Your Most Compassionate Heart the souls in Purgatory, souls who are very dear to You, and yet, who must make retribution to Your justice. May the streams of Blood and Water which gushed forth from Your Heart put out the flames of the purifying fire, that in that place, too, the power of Your mercy may be praised.

From that terrible heat of the cleansing fire
Rises a plaint to Your mercy,
And they receive comfort, refreshment, relief
In the stream of mingled Blood and Water.

Eternal Father, turn Your merciful gaze upon the souls suffering in Purgatory, who are enfolded in the Most Compassionate Heart of Jesus. I beg You, by the sorrowful Passion of Jesus Your Son, and by all the bitterness with which His most sacred Soul was flooded: Manifest Your mercy to the souls who are under Your just scrutiny. Look upon them in no other way but only through the Wounds of Jesus, Your dearly beloved Son; for we firmly believe that there is no limit to Your goodness and compassion.

Ninth Day

Today bring to Me souls who have become lukewarm, and immerse them in the abyss of My mercy. These souls wound My Heart most painfully. My soul suffered the most dreadful loathing in the Garden of Olives because of lukewarm souls. They were the reason I cried out: "Father, take this cup away from Me, if it be Your will." For them, the last hope (65) of salvation is to flee to My mercy.

Most Compassionate Jesus, You are Compassion Itself. I bring lukewarm souls into the abode of Your Most Compassionate Heart. In this fire of Your pure love let these tepid souls, who like corpses, filled You with such deep loathing, be once again set aflame. O Most Compassionate Jesus, exercise the omnipotence of Your mercy and draw them into the very ardor of Your love, and bestow upon them the gift of holy love, for nothing is beyond Your power.

Fire and ice cannot be joined,
Either the fire dies, or the ice melts.
But by Your mercy, O God,
You can make up for all that is lacking.

Eternal Father, turn Your merciful gaze upon lukewarm souls, who are nonetheless enfolded in the Most Compassionate Heart of Jesus. Father of Mercy, I beg You by the bitter Passion of Your Son and by His three-hour agony on the Cross: Let them, too, glorify the abyss of Your mercy...

O day of eternity, O day so long desired,

With thirst and longing, my eyes search you out.
Soon love will tear the veil asunder,
And you will be my salvation.

O day most beautiful, moment incomparable,
When for the first time I shall see my God,
The Bridegroom of my soul and Lord of lords,
And fear will not restrain my soul.

O day most solemn, O day of brightness,
When the soul will know God in His omnipotence
And drown totally in His love,
Knowing the miseries of exile are o'er.

O happy day, O blessed day,
When my heart will burn for You with fire eternal,
For even now I feel Your presence, though through the veil.
Through life and death, O Jesus, You are my rapture and delight.

O day, of which I dreamed through all my life,
Waiting long for You, O God,
For it is You alone whom I desire.
You are the one and only of my heart; all else is naught.

Oh day of delight, day of eternal bliss,
God of great majesty, my beloved Spouse,
You know that nothing will satisfy a virgin heart.
On Your tender Heart I rest my brow.

Appendix D
Personal Testimony of Father Ronald P. Pytel Regarding Healing of Heart Disease

Introduction to Appendix D
Personal Testimony of Father Ronald P. Pytel
Regarding Healing of Heart Disease

Father Ronald P, Pytel was the Pastor of Holy Rosary Church in Baltimore, Maryland. Father's miraculous healing of a severely damaged heart ultimately provided the Vatican with the miracle needed to canonize Blessed Faustina. Saint Faustina's life and message of Divine Mercy is shared by him.

Since the miracle for the elevation of Saint Faustina was a heart miracle Fr. Pytel's personal testimony is fascinating reading to accompany Chapter 7, *The First Miracle of Divine Mercy.*

In November of 2003, Fr. Ron Pytel lost his brief battle with cancer.

Appendix D
Personal Testimony of Father Ronald P. Pytel Regarding Healing of Heart Disease[381]

Through the Intercession of Blessed Faustina Kowalska.

My name is Father Ronald Pytel, and I am the pastor of Holy Rosary Church in Baltimore, Maryland. Our parish church is the Archdiocesan Shrine for Divine Mercy. It is also noteworthy to mention that Pope John Paul II visited and prayed in Holy Rosary Church in 1976 when he was Karol Cardinal Wojtyla. The Divine Mercy Shrine at Holy Rosary was dedicated on the first feast day of Blessed Faustina.

I have been a priest for 26 years. I was ordained at Holy Rosary Church, which is my home parish. I am of Polish ethnic background. My parents were born in America, but my grandparents came from Poland.

As a young boy, I remember seeing the Image of Divine Mercy in our school with the inscription "Jezu, ufam Tobie!" It was not until 1987, however, that I first became very well acquainted with the devotion to Divine Mercy and the chaplet while on a pilgrimage to Medjugorje.

In the Archdiocese of Baltimore, Bishop John Ricard started the Divine Mercy devotions and Mercy Sunday at the Cathedral of Mary our Queen in 1991. As the devotion grew, Holy Rosary Church became the second site for Mercy Sunday. The first Mercy Sunday Celebration at Holy Rosary was held on the day of Blessed Faustina's Beatification. On her first feast day, a permanent shrine was blessed at Holy Rosary at the spot where Cardinal Wojtyla prayed. From Blessed Faustina's first feast day until the present, we

---

381 http://www.divinemercyshrine.com/FatherPytel.html

celebrate Mercy Devotions every Second Sunday of the month at this shrine in English, every third Sunday of the month in Polish and a perpetual novena is celebrated every Thursday at noon. We also have days of recollection, pilgrimages and talks on Divine Mercy. It is interesting to note that last Mercy Sunday, devotions were celebrated in the Archdiocese of Baltimore at 37 different locations.

All of this is to give you some background information and to set the stage for my story. Throughout the winter and spring of 1995, I was suffering from what seemed like a cold and allergies. Eventually, it seemed like I had developed bronchitis. I could not get my breath when going up a flight of stairs, and I was constantly coughing. I made an appointment with a local general medical doctor who confirmed that I was suffering from allergic bronchitis. He also said, however, that my heart murmur, which I knew I had since I was a boy, seemed extremely exaggerated, and he-made an appointment for me to have a Doppler echocardiogram.

The echocardiogram was taken on June 7, 1995. It showed that my aorta was stenotic, that a calcium dome had formed over the valve, and that I was only getting about 20 % blood flow through the valve and some was backwashing. In essence, I was in cardiac heart failure. On June 8th, I had an emergency appointment with Dr. Nicholas Fortuin, an eminent cardiologist from the world-renowned Johns Hopkins Hospital in Baltimore. Dr. Fortuin is considered one of the best cardiologists in the United States. Dr. Fortuin read the echocardiogram and confirmed the stenosis of the aortic valve. He prescribed medication and sent me home for complete bed rest while he arranged for a surgical team to perform surgery at Johns Hopkins Hospital.

On the morning of June 14th, my best priest friend, Father Larry Gesy, took me to Johns Hopkins Hospital at 6:30 AM On the way to the hospital, Father Larry said to me, "Don't worry, Ron, this is all about Divine Mercy." I underwent my heart surgery at the beginning of the Novena, before the feast of the Sacred Heart of Jesus. Included in the things which I packed for the hospital stay was the Diary of Blessed Faustina. Even though I did not like the thought of cardiac surgery, I was at peace. I just knew all would be fine.

After the surgery, I was then put in cardiac intensive care until noon the next day. After the respirator and stomach drainage tubes were removed, I was moved into a private room on the cardiac floor. The nurses had me up and walking Thursday afternoon. I was released from the hospital on Monday, June 19th, five days after surgery.

During my recovery, I read the Diary of Blessed Faustina whenever I could. I also prayed the chaplet every day.

After the surgery had been performed, Dr. Peter Green, the surgeon, met with Father Larry Gesy and told him that, prior to the operation, I had suffered serious damage to the left ventricle of my heart. Since the valve was so stenotic, the left ventricle was trying to push blood which was not going through the valve; if the surgery had not been performed, I would not have lived much longer.

Shortly after leaving the hospital, I developed pleurisy on July 7th. Even though I should have been in excruciating pain, I detected something was wrong only because I developed a fever. I had no pain. I was re-admitted to the hospital with a liter of fluid on my left lung. My lung was drained of the fluid. I was given antibiotics and observed as blood cultures were taken to make sure that there was no infection going to the heart. When the doctors were sure I was out of danger, and my oral medication was regulated, I was discharged from the hospital. My normal weight of about 165 pounds had dropped to 144 pounds. I looked like the victim of a concentration camp.

Gradually during July and August, I regained some weight and strength. I visited Dr. Fortuin in August. After the examination, Father Larry Gesy who had accompanied me had his examination. Fr. Larry discussed my situation at length with Dr. Fortuin who said that he did not know what kind of life I would be able to resume. He did not think that I would resume any normal schedule. He also said I was un-insurable. My longevity was certainly shortened, and Dr. Fortuin's prognosis was not optimistic. The damage to the left ventricle was quite serious. The situation had been pushed to the maximum before surgery. I had indeed been in congestive heart failure which was masked by what I thought were allergies and bronchitis. Father Larry was startled and shocked by this information. Fr. Larry gradually shared the prognosis with me.

I returned to the parish in early September. I was, however, on a restricted schedule.

On October 5th, we celebrated an all day vigil before the Blessed Sacrament with prayers, chaplet of Divine Mercy, Rosary and talks on our Lord's Gift of Mercy. The day concluded with a concelebrated Mass. All of this was in preparation for the Holy Father's visit to Baltimore on October 8th. I was the celebrant of the Mass. I spoke about trust and how I felt the Lord was touching me with his mercy. Physically, I was feeling and looking somewhat better. That evening, a group of individuals who have a ministry entitled "Our Father's Work", prayed over me for continued healing. Blessed Faustina was invoked to join in the prayer, and I venerated a first class relic of Blessed Faustina. During the prayer, I rested in the Holy Spirit. I laid on the floor for about 15 minutes. I was totally conscious and awake, but I could not move. I felt like I was paralyzed as the healing ministry and my parishioners gathered around me and prayed. Later that evening, I realized that I had forgotten to take my heart medication. I took the medication around midnight, and was relaxing before going to bed. I began to have chest discomforts when I took a deep breath.

Up until this time, I had no chest pains except from the incision in the chest after surgery. This was something new. I felt that I probably had been too active that day.

This pain was present every day after that, but it would be stronger at certain times during the day. The following Sunday, when the Holy Father visited Baltimore, our bus was parked 1.6 kilometers from the stadium. After the Mass, two people were missing from the bus. One person was my mother. I ran between the bus and the stadium five or six times looking for the missing people. I experienced no trouble breathing, and it was a very warm October day.

The pain persisted every day, and I decided to take some time to retreat at the ocean. While I was there, I realized that the pain was the strongest after I took the heart medication. The next day, I did not take the medication, and there was no pain.

I called Dr. Fortuin and told him of the problem. I felt that the heart medication, zestril, which he had prescribed for me, caused the problem. Dr. Fortuin told me that this was the best possible medication for my heart condition, and that I had already tolerated the medication for 2 months with no reaction. He told me, however, that if I felt that my body was telling me something, to try alternating between a half dosage and a full dosage to see if that helped and to call him in a week. The half dosage was better. The pain was less severe and dissipated more quickly. I called Dr. Fortuin and told him the results, and he told me to stay on the half dosage until my appointment with him in 9 days.

On November 9th, I once again visited Dr. Fortuin for a scheduled appointment. After an initial examination, a Doppler echocardiogram was taken. Dr. Fortuin viewed the results of the test and then called me into his office. He stared at me in silence for what seemed like an eternity and then he spoke. To the best of my recollection, these were his exact words: "Ron, someone has intervened for you." I asked, "what do you mean?" he said: "Your heart is normal." I said "What?" And he repeated, "Your heart is normal." I responded, "Well, Dr. Green, the surgeon had suggested that you do an echocardiogram to see if the left ventricle was strengthening.' And Dr. Fortuin said, "No, no ... we're talking normal. I was not at all optimistic about your condition. I can't explain it." He continued, "You have no restrictions, you are to take no medication except the Coumadin, and I'll see you in a year." I responded, "A year?" he said, "Yeah, a year. Your heart is normal."

Dr. Fortuin then reminded me that I needed the blood thinners because of the artificial valve, and to continue to get my blood-clotting factor checked every month so he could check the dosage. He told me to discontinue the fluid pills, potassium and zestril.

Upon leaving the doctor's office, I called Fr. Larry Gesy and told him what Dr. Fortuin had said. Father Larry's response was "Well, I guess we got the miracle we prayed for." In November of 1996, a formal Tribunal was held in the Archdiocese of Baltimore to acquire sworn depositions from the doctors and other witnesses about the change in my health. On December 8th, Fr. Seraphim Michalenko, vice-postulator for America, arrived in Baltimore. I should note that December 8th, the Feast of the Immaculate Conception, was a favorite feast day for Blessed Faustina because the Blessed Mother had appeared to her on that day. On December 9th, Fr. Seraphim went to the Baltimore Tribunal where the documents were sealed and packaged. Then he, Fr. Larry Gesy and I boarded a plane for Rome. The documents numbered over 800 pages in medical records, and about 500 pages of sworn depositions.

Divine Mercy Shrine
Holy Rosary Church
408 South Chester Street
Baltimore, Maryland 21231

Bibliography

Andrasz, S.J., Joseph, *Divine Mercy...We Trust in You!* (Stockbridge, MA: Marian Helpers, 1986)

Aquinas, St. Thomas, *Summa Theologiae* (Garden City, NY: Image Books, 1969)

Barbet, M.D., Pierre, *A Doctor at Calvary* (Garden City, NY: Image Books, 1963)

Barclay, William, *The Apostles' Creed for Everyman* (New York, NY: Harper & Row, 1967)

Brown, S. S., Raymond E. and Joseph A. Fitzmyer, S. J., Roland E. Murphy, O. Carm., Editors, *The Jerome Biblical Commentary* (Englewood Cliffs, NJ: Prentice-Hall, Inc., 1968)

"Burial and Burial Customs," *The Universal Jewish Encyclopedia*, 1940

Catechism of the Catholic Church, Libreria Editrice Vaticana, 1997

Cirrincione, Msgr. Joseph A., and Thomas A. Nelson. *The Rosary and the Crisis of Faith* (Rockford, IL: TAN Books, 1986)

Conference transcription from a talk that Father John Hardon gave to the Institute on Religious Life, Chapter VIII, Christology of Thomas Aquinas found at http://www.therealpresence.org/archives/Christology

Dubay, S.M., Thomas, *The Fire Within* (San Francisco, CA: Ignatius Press, 1989)

Faustina Kowalska, Sister M., *Divine Mercy in My Soul, Diary*, (Stockbridge, MA: Marian Press 1987)

Gospel of Nicodemus

Green, Joel B., and Scot McKnight, I. Howard Marshall, Editors, *Dictionary of Jesus and the Gospels* (Downers Grove, IL: Intervarsity Press, 1992)

Guscin, Mark, *The Oviedo Cloth* (Cambridge, England: The Lutterworth Press, 1998)

Jacobus de Voragine, O.P, Blessed, *The Golden Legend: Readings on the Saints*

Johnson, Kevin Orlin, *Why Do Catholics Do That?* (New York, NY: Ballantine, 1994)

John Paul II, *Dives in Misericordia* (Boston, MA: Daughters of St. Paul, 1980)

Kosicki, Fr. George, *Now is the Time for Mercy* (Stockbridge, MA: Marian Helpers, 1993)

L'Osservatore Romano, Weekly Edition in English, 3 May 2000

Lukefahr, C.M., Father Oscar, *A Catholic Guide to the Bible* (Liguori, MO: Liguori Press, 1992)

Mahzor Vitri

Maloney, S.J., George A., *God's Incredible Mercy* (New York, NY: Alba House, 1989)

Michalenko, Fr. Seraphim, "The Wombs of Mercy," *The Association of Marian Helpers Bulletin*, Summer 1995

_____ "The Holy Shroud and the Image of The Divine Mercy According to blessed Faustina Kowalska," *The Holy Face Symposium* (Rome, Italy, October 1999)

Michalenko, C.M.G.T., Sister Sophia, *The Life of Faustina Kowalska* (Ann Arbor, MI: Servant Publications, 1999)

Miller, John D., *Beads & Prayers,* (London: Burns & Oates, 2002) *Mingana*,. Christian documents in Syriac, Arabic, and Garshuni with two introductions by Rendel Harris. Woodbrooke Studies, Vol. 2. Cambridge: W. Heffer & Sons, 1928

Montefiore, C. G., *The Synoptic Gospels*, (New York, NY: KTAV Publishing House, 1968)

Murphy, O. P., Richard T. A., *Background to the Bible*, (Ann Arbor, MI: Servant Books, 1978)

McGrath, Msgr. William C., "The Lady of the Rosary" in *A Woman Clothed With the Sun,* (Garden City, NY: Image Books, 1961)

Odell, Catherine M., *Faustina: Apostle of Divine Mercy* (Huntington, IN: Our Sunday Visitor, 1998) *Those Who Saw Her,* (Huntington, IN: Our Sunday Visitor, 1995)

Parente, Pietro, et al. *Dictionary of Dogmatic Theology* (Milwaukee, WI: Bruce Publishing Company, 1952)

Ratzinger, Joseph Cardinal, *The Spirit of the Liturgy* (San Francisco, CA: Ignatius Press, 2000)

Shakespeare, William, *The Merchant of Venice.*

Scott, Bruce, *The Feasts of Israel* (Bellmawr, NJ: The Friends of Israel Gospel Ministry, Inc. 1997)

Shaw, Russell, editor, *Our Sunday Visitor's Encyclopedia of Catholic Doctrine* (Huntington, IN: Our Sunday Visitor, 1997)

Sopocko, Fr. Michael, The "Summarium," p. 95, No. 251, in transcripts faxed to Life Foundation Ministries from the National Shrine of Divine Mercy, Stockbridge, MA 03/15/97 from Fr. Seraphim Michalenko, Vice Postulator of the Canonization of Blessed Faustina Kowalska.

_____ "The Matter of Correctness of the Image of Divine Mercy," *Pillars of Fire in My Soul* (Stockbridge, MA: Marian Press, 2003)

Stevenson, Kenneth E., and Gary R. Habermas, *Verdict on the Shroud,* (Ann Arbor, MI: Servant Publications. 1981)

Tarnawska, Maria, *Sister Faustina Kowalska—Her Life and Mission* (Stockbridge, MA: Marian Helpers, 1989)

Teresa of Avila, "The Life," *The Collected Works of St. Teresa*, translated by Kieran Kavanaugh and Otilio Rodriguez (Washington, DC: ICS Publications, 1976)

The Catholic Encyclopedia, Robert C. Broderick, editor, (Nashville, KY: Thomas Nelson Publisher. 1986)

The Documents of Vatican II, Walter M. Abbott, S.J., General Editor (New York, NY: The American Press 1966)

The Letters of Saint Faustina, translated by Sr. M. Beata Piekut O.L.M., (Cracow, Poland: Misericordia Publications, 2007)

The New Jerusalem Bible, (Garden City, NY: Darton, Longman & Todd, Ltd., and Doubleday & Company, Inc. 1985)

The New Saint Joseph Missal (New York, NY: The Catholic Book Publishing Company. 1959)

Throckmorton, Jr., Burton H., *Gospel Parallels: A Synopsis of the First Three Gospels,* (New York, NY: Thomas Nelson, Inc., 1973)

Whanger, Mary and Alan, *The Shroud of Turin* (Franklin, TN: Providence House Publishers, 1978)

CPSIA information can be obtained at www.ICGtesting.com
Printed in the USA
LVOW062313030412

276015LV00002B/2/P